Knitting
Board
Basics

Pat Novak & Kim Novak

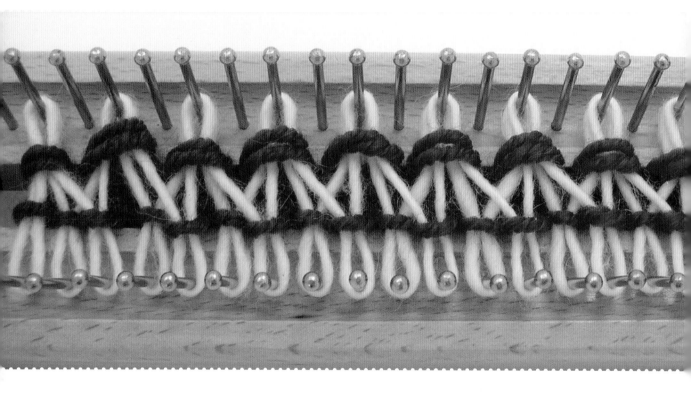

ST. MARTIN'S GRIFFIN
NEW YORK

Knitting Board
Basics

A Beginner's Guide to Using a Knitting Board
with Over 30 Easy Projects

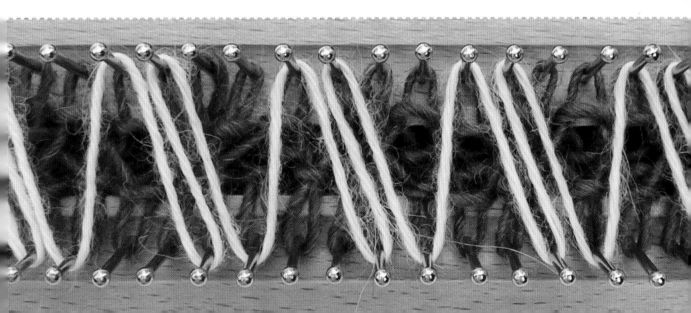

www.stmartins.com

Photographs on pages 7, 9, 10, 11, 13–44, 48–50, 53, 55–57, 59, 64, 66–71, 73, 79–84, 86, 91, 94, 119, 122, 123, 129, 130, 131, 154, 159 are copyright © 2010 by Ivan de Petrovsky. Photographs on pages 87, 88, 96, 108, 110, 115, 117, 121, 124, 128, 132, 135, 136, 152, 155, 156, 160, 163, 164, 167, 173, 174–177 are copyright © 2010 by Dennis Welsh. Photographs on pages 2, 3, 45, 47, 51, 52, 65–66, 74, 75, 76, 77, 106, 145 are copyright © 2010 by Pat Novak and Kim Novak. Photographs on pages 102, 104, 140, 151, 169, 170 are copyright © 2010 by Dave Gilk. Photographs on pages 92, 127, 148 are copyright © 2010 by Peter Leighton. Photograph on page 112 is copyright © 2010 by Ryuji Syzuki.

BOOK DESIGN BY WOOLYPEAR

Library of Congress Cataloging-in-Publication Data

Novak, Pat.
    Knitting board basics : a beginner's guide to using a knitting board with over 30
easy projects / Pat Novak and Kim Novak.—1st ed.
        p. cm.
    Includes index.
    ISBN 978-0-312-58254-8
    1. Knitting—Patterns. 2. Hand looms. I. Novak, Kim, 1968- II. Title.
    TT825.N78 2010
    746.43'2041—dc22   2009046748

First Edition: August 2010

10 9 8 7 6 5 4 3 2

Contents

INTRODUCTION
My Story

I find myself thinking back to that day in Los Angeles when I first walked into a yarn store. It wasn't really a yarn store, only a little section of a variety store where I picked up my first ball of yarn. I had decided to teach myself how to knit. So with two sets of knitting needles and a couple balls of yarn, off I went. Pattern? No, not me: "Just use your imagination," I thought. After several ill-fitting items that I can't even remember now, I decided to try a pattern. I was nineteen years old and totally fascinated with what I was learning, creating, and really enjoying.

All the varieties of yarn and the endless possibilities of things to create were enough to keep me excited for a long time. The way knitting touched my deepest creative sensibilities was so amazing to me. I discovered true relaxation and peace when I was knitting.

Soon, every waking, available minute was spent with my yarn and needles. Everyone I knew was awarded a hand-knit sweater, and each masterpiece turned out quite well. At least, at that time, they looked "good" to me. I can't say that I have recently seen any of my original pieces in anyone's closet. Well, that was a long time ago.

Discovering the Knitting Board was quite accidental. My daughter Kim purchased some double-knit sweaters on one of her many trips abroad. She asked the local crafters how these garments were knit to be so warm and cozy. The story of an antiquated knitting tool emerged. It was simply two sticks of wood with wood pins hammered into them, fixed parallel to one another. To use it, the knitter wrapped the yarn around the different pegs in various patterns. Kim not only bought the sweaters; she brought the knitting contraption home for me to see, being the "experienced knitter" that I was.

We were both intrigued and had several additional looms created by a local woodworker. Our fascination with the double knit created on these looms led us both to jump in and start making handcrafted double-knit coats and sweaters. It was a great hobby, and we had a wonderful time learning together whenever Kim came to visit me in Tennessee or I visited her in Connecticut. However, that hobby soon turned into a small business that grew very quickly, and we were soon taking orders for our warm double-knit sweaters.

Through this business of selling our knitwear, we found that our customers were interested in our knitting tool—the Knitting Board. They wanted to learn to make their own sweaters, hats, scarves, and coats as we were doing. That seemed like a great idea to us—let's teach everyone who would like to learn this wonderful craft of knitting with a board loom. Our local woodworkers obliged us by making several new knitting boards according to our specifications. The engineering of the board evolved over the next few years, as we refined the proportions and contours to those we use today.

It's been most satisfying to watch our newfound hobby/business grow and expand as more and more people became passionate about using Knitting Boards and looms. So many people are jumping into the movement and finding that working with a Knitting Board is fun and easy. They are catching the fever.

The knitting board frame is not a new concept. References to its existence go back to the mid-sixteenth century. In his 1879 book *Die Strassburger Tucher-und Weberzunft*, Gustav von Schmoller mentions that the *Stuhl*, or knitting loom, was used in textile guilds in Strasburg, Germany, in 1535. It is also possible that the Silesian and Alsatian carpets of the seventeenth and eighteenth centuries were made on such boards. So even though there are not a lot of details about the original knitting looms, just the mention of them tells us that they existed and were used for creating textiles and garments.

Today there are many different types of looms available to knitters—some are made out of wood and some out of plastic. There are round, oval, square, and double-sided looms. There are looms with a single row of needles referred to as a "rake" and ones with a double row of needles that create a double-sided or double knit fabric. For the purpose of this book, we will be exploring the world of knitting boards that are used to create a double-sided and reversible hand-knit fabric.

At one time, women knit to keep their families warm. Today, we make hand-knit clothing and home accessories for the pleasure of the craft and the joy of giving something so special to our loved ones. As a society, our usual means of producing almost everything has evolved from handmade to

machine-made—and in reaction, many of us want to "make it ourselves." We want it to knit up easily and quickly. We want it to look professional yet be hand-made. Working with a knitting board is truly an art and a craft that can be enjoyed by experienced and new knitters of all ages, including young children and teens. It's a hobby, an art, a revenue stream, an addiction, and an absolute love affair.

When a beloved hobby like knitting grows in a new direction, devotees want to check it out and see what all the excitement is about. Although loom knitting has been around in one form or another for several hundred years, it's only recently that we've seen explosive interest in it as a leisure craft. The ranks of new loom knitters are swelling because it's so easy to learn to use a knitting board. Traditional knitters who have limited hand flexibility enjoy returning to a favorite hobby, free of pain and awkwardness. The knitting board can be enjoyed by young and old alike—men, women, and children experience so much fun, relaxation, creative expression, and satisfaction when working with yarns to create beautiful, useful items. It makes us feel good to see this happen and to know we helped bring it about.

Pat Novak

The Basics

How does a knitting board work, and what can you do with one? The first part of this book explains the mechanics of the board and the many basic techniques you can master to produce wonderful knitting. You'll learn everything from how to put stitches on the board to how to add fringe or a pompom to your finished work; from how to work many different stitches and create multicolored patterns to how to shape your work and put the pieces together.

How a Knitting Board Works

A Knitting Board is a hand-knitting tool that creates a double-knit fabric—a two-layer fabric that is finished and, in most cases, identical on both sides. There is no wrong side. Compared with single-knit fabric—where one side, the knit side, is smooth and the reverse side, the purl side, is ridged—double knitting creates two interlocked layers that are smooth on both sides (the purl ridges face each other between the layers).

A knitting board offers a much faster way to create double-knit fabric than conventional two-needle knitting does. It is very versatile, and by changing the gauge (the number of stitches per inch) or the stitch pattern, you can create many different looks and use all types of yarn. You can shape the work by increasing or decreasing the number of stitches, just as you do in conventional knitting, and your project stays right on the board while you do this. The project possibilities are endless—from very simple items made of squares and rectangles to more complex sweaters with intricate design.

The knitting board, sometimes called a *long loom*, features two long, narrow wood or plastic strips (referred to as *boards*), positioned parallel to one another at a fixed or adjustable distance, with a space between them through which the knit fabric passes as it is created. Each board is studded with a row of upright *needles*—well, they're really pegs, but they're referred to as needles (boards have pegs of wood, plastic, or metal). The needles on one board lie directly across from those on the opposite board. Each pair of opposite needles creates one stitch. Thus, a knitting board with fifty needles on each board will make a fabric with up to fifty stitches. This is important to understand when you start working, because most often, what you do on one needle will be repeated on the other needle of the same stitch. There will be some exceptions to that rule.

The Process

The process of knitting on a knitting board is a simple weave-and-hook movement across the two rows of needles, back and forth, from one board to the other. The pattern of the weaving—the sequence in which the yarn is wrapped from needle to needle—creates the different stitches. After the yarn is woven as specified there are at least two loops passing around each needle; a special kind of hook, called a *knit hook*, is used to lift the lower loop over the top one, forming a stitch that drops off the needle into the space between the two boards. Because the yarn consistently passes from one board to the other, the stitches on the boards are interlocked, forming a double-knit fabric rather than the single knit created with conventional knitting needles or a rake (a single-sided loom).

For all instructions in this book, when we refer to the *back of the board* or the *top board*, we mean the board that is farthest away from you while you work. When we refer to the *front of the board* or the *bottom board*, we mean the board that is closest to you. Being right- or left-handed is not an important issue. When we weave, we work from left to right. If you are more comfortable working from right to left, that is fine.

BOARD KNITTING AT A GLANCE

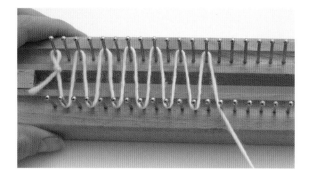

Start with a loop knot as your first stitch. Place the loop on the first needle to be used for the project. Weave yarn back and forth across the two rows of needles to be used.

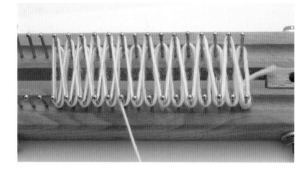

Weave again so that all the working needles have a second row of loops.

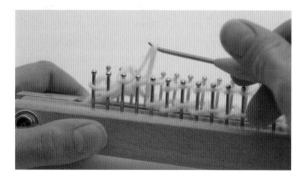

Now hook the second row of loops over the first (or lower) row of loops and lift the loops off the board. This leaves one row of loops on the needles and completes the first row of knitting. Weave yarn across the rows of needles again and then hook over again.

This is referred to as simply, "weave and hook." You continue to work the stitches row by row until the piece reaches the desired length. As the knitted fabric grows, it drops down between the two boards. Once the piece is completed, you remove the knitted fabric from the board by binding off.

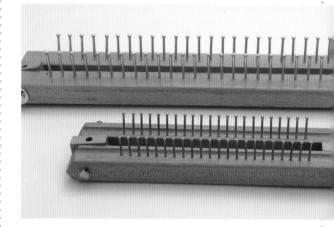

SELECTING YOUR KNITTING BOARD

Knitting boards come in a variety of sizes with different options. The type you use dictates the gauge (or gauges) in which you can work. *Gauge* is the number of stitches per inch and the number of rows per inch in the finished fabric. On some boards, the distance between the two boards is fixed, or *stationary*; on others, it is adjustable. Both types come in several lengths, and the number, size, and spacing of the needles vary as well. The stationary type is the most common and, depending on the relative spacing of the boards and their needles, can be classified as fine gauge, small gauge, regular gauge, or large gauge. An adjustable knitting board can be configured to allow you to work in several or all of these gauges.

Choosing the right knitting board is like picking out the best car to suit your lifestyle. The question becomes "What do I want to create and which board will do the best job?" Most knitting looms and boards come with their own instructions and some basic patterns designed for that particular product.

Before you first purchase a knitting board, it's smart to look around and see what kinds of fabric can be made on each type of board and the sorts of items those fabrics are good for. Do you like knitting that is chunky with large stitches? Then maybe a board with an inch or more between needles will work for you. If the needles are very close together and the board is labeled *fine gauge*, you'll be able to use only very fine yarn—no matter how many needles there are. Consider how many stitches and how wide of a piece of knitting the board will be able to create. Also, think about the weight of the board and how you will be working on it: If you want something portable, then you should think about keeping it shorter than 24 inches. If you're planning on staying at home with it—or taking it to a knitting group and making large-scale items like one-piece afghans—you should look at something longer, up to 40 inches. The most versatile knitting board will be one that has adjustable spacing between the boards and can be used with yarns of all weights. Once you're hooked on this kind of knitting, you may want to invest in several different boards.

Determining the Board Gauge

If you are familiar with conventional two-needle knitting, you know that needles come in many sizes and that their size affects the size of the stitch you make. With conventional knitting, you can change to larger or smaller needles to make larger or smaller stitches. You can't change the size of the needles on a knitting board—whatever is there is the only option on that board. The size of the stitch is determined by the distance between the needles on each board and the spacing between the two boards. With a stationary board, the only way to change the gauge is by using thicker or thinner yarn or by skipping needles at a regular interval when you weave. With an adjustable knitting board, you can increase or decrease the distance between the paired boards, which facilitates more variation in the size of the stitch created.

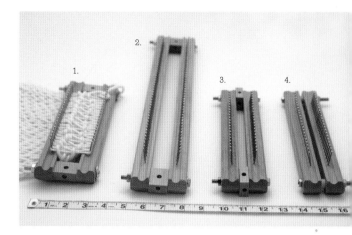

These knitting boards have wider or narrower spacing between each set of boards, which allows you to determine which spacing is the best choice for the yarn and stitch pattern chosen. Generally patterns recommend which spacing should be used.

#1 has 1¼-inch spacing between the boards. This produces a very open weave knit. It is also used when working with very bulky yarn.

#2 has 1-inch spacing. This also allows for a more open weave. It is generally used when working with thick loopy boucle yarns or hairy fibers.

#3 has the standard setting used on most knitting boards. This produces a solid knit with worsted weight yarns.

#4 has a narrower setting. This creates a tighter knit. It is generally used when working dishcloths or baby items when working with finer weight yarns.

Using the wider settings may require longer bolts (these are used to hold the boards together), so be sure to check your particular knitting board for instructions on how to adjust for wider spacing between the two boards.

CHOOSING YARN

Before starting, choose the appropriate yarn for your project. Project patterns usually suggest using a specific yarn and include a photo of the project completed in that yarn. Often you will also be directed to some alternative yarn choices. If you are new to a knitting board, you will want to focus on mastering techniques and stitches; this is easier to do with a basic yarn than one with a hairy or loopy texture, which often makes the stitches difficult to see. New knitters often find yarn that is extremely slippery, hairy, loopy, or fuzzy to be a bit more difficult to manipulate, so you might want to save these until you're confident about the basic knitting process.

We recommend starting with a nice single-ply, worsted-weight yarn. This can be wool, acrylic, or a blend of several fibers. Many basic yarns include a bit of mohair, which gives them a nice soft feel, and these are fine as long as they're not overly hairy or fragile. Once you know how to work the stitches, you can experiment with fine yarns to make open, airy knit fabrics. Or you may want to try a thick yarn to create a firmer, denser fabric. Remember, you can create many looks on one board just by varying the yarns with which you work.

Spend some time in a local yarn shop or craft center and explore the wonderful world of fibers. The colors available are awesome and absolutely alluring. There's a lot of terminology with which you should become familiar, and we can cover just some of the basics here: Yarn weights range from fine to very chunky. They are usually labeled as, from thinnest to thickest: *fingering, baby, DK* (double knit), *worsted, bulky,* and *chunky.* Each comes in various *plies,* which simply refers to the number of strands twisted together to form the yarn. Some have a tight twist and some a very soft, loose twist. You'll also see some novelty yarns that are "thick-and-thin," bouclé, hairy, or even twined with metallic fibers. Sometimes you'll see a fine yarn twisted with a very soft strand of unspun fiber, or *roving.* If you decide to use a yarn other than the one recommended in your project directions or are working without a pattern, be sure to make a test swatch, as explained in the next section.

3 sts = 1 inch

Check the Stitch Gauge

Most patterns will give you the knitting gauge required to make a piece come out to a specified size. It is always wise to do a test swatch, measure across a row, and count the number of stitches that equal 1 inch, so you can be sure you are getting the desired gauge in your chosen yarn. If you are not working from a pattern, a gauge swatch will enable you to calculate how many stitches you'll need to make a piece the size you want: For instance, let's say you plan to knit a scarf. No pattern is really needed. Instead, make a test swatch of 10 stitches in your favorite yarn and knit it to be about 4 inches long. Then measure across the piece with a ruler and count the number of stitches in 1 inch. The result is the gauge—if you count 3 stitches in 1 inch, your gauge is 3 stitches to the inch.

To figure out how many stitches you need, multiply the gauge by the width desired for your scarf. If you want to make a 10-inch-wide scarf, multiply 10 by 3 for a total of 30 stitches. Once you have 30 stitches on the board (how to do this is explained later; see Casting On, page 20), you can knit the scarf to whatever length you like and it will be complete. Or you can also count the number of rows there are in 1 inch of your swatch (measure lengthwise for this) and use the result to calculate how many rows you'll need to work for the scarf to be a specific length. Say you find there are 4 rows in 1 inch, and you want your scarf to end up 50 inches long: Multiply 50 by 4 to learn you'll need to work 200 rows.

By making a swatch like the ones shown here, you will also be able to see the way the yarn looks and feels when knitted at a particular setting or in a particular stitch. If you feel that you would like a more open, looser effect for your scarf, adjust the board to put more space between the two rows of needles, or use a thinner yarn, or choose a different stitch. Each of these options will produce fewer stitches per inch—a smaller gauge.

2.5 sts = 1 inch

PREPARING TO KNIT

You can work with a knitting board almost anywhere, so pick your favorite spot—whether that's a cozy chair in your home, the local coffee shop, at a group knit-out, or in the car (while someone else drives). Find a comfortable position for holding your board. Most knitters find the process works best when they lay the board across their lap, the arms of a chair, or on a tabletop. This is all a matter of individual preference. You will find your best position.

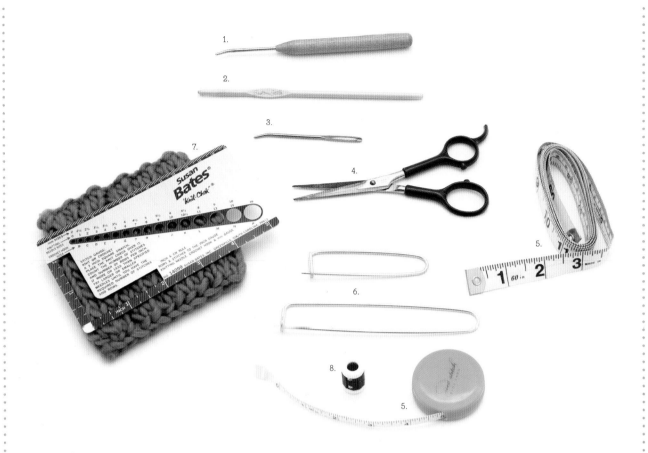

Before you take your first turn at a board or start a project, assemble the supplies you'll use. It's handy to keep a little bucket or basket of tools prepared and ready for knitting. Here are the things you'll need; with the exception of the knitting board and pattern, they're pictured above.

Knitting board with Pattern. Choose one that gives the right gauge for your project.

1. **Knit hook**, to lift loops up and over the needles. This is usually a small, slightly curved metal hook or prong with a comfortable handle. Several varieties are available.

2. **Crochet hook**, for finishing work. It's good to have several sizes, to match the weight of different yarns, on hand.

3. Large darning or **yarn needle**, to sew seams when joining two knitted pieces.

4. Small pair of **scissors**, for cutting yarn.

5. **Tape measures**. Flexible flat and retractable types are both useful.

6. **Stitch holders**. These keep your work from unraveling if you need to remove it from the board.

7. **Gauge measure**—a special ruler that has a window for counting stitch and row gauges (and, usually, holes for checking the size of crochet hooks and conventional knitting needles).

8. **Row counter**. This revolving gauge for recording the number of rows or stitches you have worked is especially handy for complex patterns.

Casting On

Casting on is the process of putting stitches on the knitting board. A single stitch on the knitting board consists of the yarn loops on two needles that are directly across from each other on the two boards—one needle on the front board and another opposite it on the back board. For instance, if a pattern calls for you to cast on twenty stitches, you will cast on over twenty needles on the front board and twenty needles on the back board. Your project may require only a few of the needles on the board or the entire span. Where on the board you begin the cast-on depends on what you are making and the number of needles you're using. You will, most of the time, start with an even number of stitches. Many patterns are available with detailed instructions for specific items, but you may enjoy figuring out your own designs using your creativity and a little math.

There are several methods for placing the stitches on the board; here we will look at the three that are most useful and versatile: *Cast On with Anchor Yarn*, *Cast On with Design 8*, and *Cast On with Basic 8*. Some project directions tell you which cast-on method to use, but sometimes you will want to choose the one you think will work best. You may also cast on using some of the different knitting stitches (see Cast On in Pattern, page 25), and many of the projects in this book begin that way. A cool thing about the knitting board is that no matter which cast-on method you use, the edge stitches will be locked together as the piece moves off the needles and down between the boards—they may look loose, but they won't unravel!

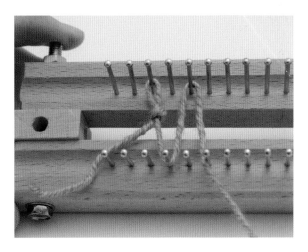

Make a loop knot with a 2- to 4-inch tail and place it on the starting needle of the top board; this can be the needle at the left end or anywhere else, as long as there are enough needles to its right to accommodate the number of stitches you need. Weave the yarn down, around the second needle from the left on the bottom board (skipping the needle directly opposite your starting needle), and then back up and around the third needle on the top board.

tip:

When you begin, make the loop knot the size of a pencil if you're using a fine yarn and a little larger when using a bulky yarn.

Cast On with Anchor Yarn

This method of casting on gives a very neat and even edge. It uses the same weave pattern as Stockinette Stitch (page 27), the most basic knitting stitch. It incorporates an anchor yarn, which secures the beginning of the work and minimizes the amount of stretch in the cast-on edge. The anchor yarn is also handy for pulling your work down between the boards when you begin; it is usually removed when the work is finished. You can use any sturdy yarn for the anchor unless the project directions indicate that it will remain in the finished work, in which case it should be the same yarn used for the rest of the project. Your first few rows may look a little loose and loopy, but when your knitting is finished the edge will be very even and secure. Use this cast-on method when you want an edge that doesn't stretch a lot—the top of a bag or a rug border, for instance, or for a firm hem and cuffs on a sweater.

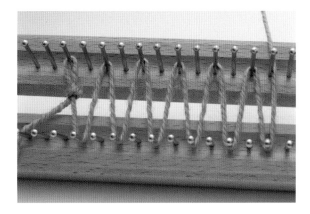

Continue to weave back and forth, around the outside of every other needle on each board, until you have wrapped the desired number of needles. Pass the yarn straight across the board on the outside (to the right) of the needle opposite the last wrapped needle on the front board.

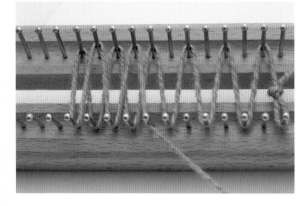

Turn the board around and repeat the process back to the beginning, this time weaving around the needles you skipped the first time.

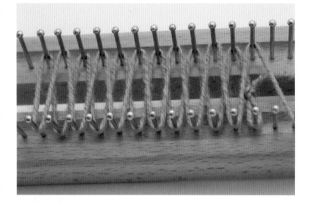

The last needle to be wrapped is directly across from the needle with the loop knot. Now all your needles on both boards have one loop.

tip:

If your anchor yarn is to remain in the finished project as a drawstring, and the yarn you're using is very fine or flimsy, use a double strand for the anchor.

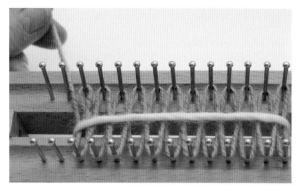

Now it's time to add the anchor yarn: Cut a piece of sturdy yarn about three times the length of the stitches on the board. Lay the yarn across the stitches, between the rows of needles, and let the ends hang down between the boards. Tie the ends together under the board, so that the yarn is loose.

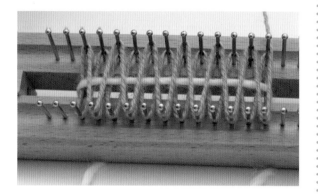

Turn the board around again. Pass the yarn up and around the needle with the loop knot and then, in the same sequence as before, weave the yarn around alternate needles again.

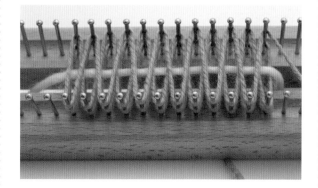

Turn the board around once more and weave back to the beginning, wrapping the skipped needles.

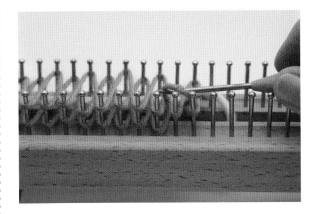

To secure the yarn, hook over the last needle wrapped. This will keep the yarn from coming unwrapped. Then hook from left to right about halfway across the front board, lifting the lower loop on each needle up and over the needle from the outside of the board. When you get to the middle, stop. Then go to the first needle at the right end of the front board and hook from right to left until you reach the middle again. Now turn the board and do the same thing on the back board, hooking from left to right to the middle, and then from right to left. Be sure to hook over each needle. Now all needles have only one loop, and your stitches are cast on.

Once you have hooked over all the needles, gently pull down on the anchor yarn to secure the stitches. If some loose loops remain, especially in the center of knitting, rest assured that they will tighten once you have three or four rows complete and the fabric hangs below the board. You can tug the anchor yarn down after or during each row of knitting. To see how to remove the anchor yarn and finish the cast-on edge, turn to page 66.

tip:

You can use an anchor yarn with any type of cast-on and any stitch weave pattern (see Cast On in Pattern, page 25).

Cast On with Design 8

This method of casting on gives a finished edge that mirrors the stretch of the knit fabric yet offers some stability. It works really well for hems that you'd like to stretch or for the edges of hats. This cast-on takes only one complete pass on the board.

Make a loop knot with a 2- to 4-inch tail and place it on the starting needle of the back board. Bring the yarn down to the front board, to the right of the needle directly across from the starting needle. Wrap the yarn clockwise and pass it back to the right of the needle on the back board, creating a figure eight across the boards.

Wrap the same needles again, passing the yarn counterclockwise around the back needle and clockwise around the front one. This places two loops on each of the first two needles.

Using your fingers to keep tension on the working end of the yarn, hook the lower loop over the needle on the front board.

Hook the lower loop over the needle on the back board. You now have only one loop on these two needles. Pull the yarn snugly to reduce any slack in the working yarn. Now wrap the figure eight twice around the next pair of needles, just as you did for the first stitch; for this cast-on method, you don't skip needles. Hook over these two needles and pull the yarn to tighten.

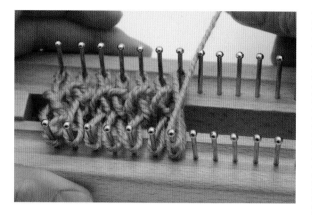

Continue to wrap the double figure eight and hook over the paired stitches as you go, until you've cast on the desired number.

Cast On with Basic 8

This method of casting on is great when you want a very loose edge—for instance, when making a lacy fabric, where a tight edge would look too structured. This edge doesn't have any tension and will stretch as much as the knitting itself. It creates a lacy finish that makes the fabric look very soft and flowing.

Make a loop knot with a 3- to 4-inch tail and place it on the starting needle of the back board. Bring the yarn down to the front board, to the right of the needle directly across from the starting needle. Wrap clockwise and pass to the back board again, placing the yarn to the right of the second needle, as shown.

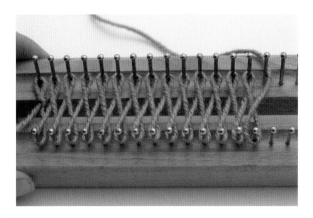

Wrap the yarn counterclockwise around the second needle on the back board. Bring it back down to the right of the second needle on the front board and wrap clockwise. Continue to weave back and forth in this pattern until you have wrapped the desired number of needles, ending on the lower front board.

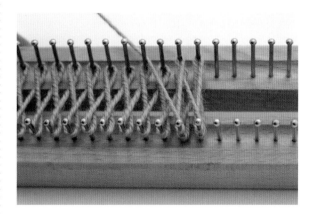

Now pass the yarn straight back and wrap it clockwise around the last needle on the back board, so that there are two loops on that needle. Bring the yarn forward and wrap it counterclockwise around the last needle on the front board. Continue to wrap the needles in reverse sequence, wrapping clockwise around all the back needles and counterclockwise around the front ones.

Optional: You may add an anchor yarn at this point to assist you to 'pull down' the first 3-4 rows easily.

To secure the yarn, hook over the last needle wrapped. This will keep the yarn from coming unwrapped. Then hook from left to right about halfway across the front board, lifting the lower loop on each needle up and over the needle from the outside of the board. When you get to the middle, stop. Then go to the first needle at the right end of the front board and hook from right to left until you reach the middle again. Now turn the board and do the same thing on the back board, hooking from left to right to the middle, and then from right to left. Be sure to hook over each needle. Now all needles have only one loop, and your stitches are cast on.

Cast On in Pattern

There are various stitches that give knitted fabric a distinctive appearance (see the Stitches chapter, page 26), and several of them can be used for casting on. Depending on the project you're making, casting on in a specific stitch can enhance the look or fluidity of the knitted edge. In fact, some of the projects in this book indicate that this should be done. Stitches that work well for casting on are Stockinette (page 27), Rib (page 30), Open Braid (page 34), Loopy Rib (page 35), and Crisscross (page 39); to cast on in one of them, simply weave one complete circular of the stitch, lay an anchor yarn, weave another complete circular of the stitch, and then hook over.

Stitches

The process of wrapping the yarn from one needle to another is called weaving. The path used to weave the yarn can be varied in order to create different textures, which we call pattern stitches. Using different stitches is fun and interesting and adds great character to your work. Our favorites are explained in this chapter. They include:

Stockinette Stitch	Double Rib Stitch
Purl Stitch	Loopy Rib Stitch
Rib Stitch	Zigzag Stitch
Open Rib Stitch	Crisscross Stitch
Open Braid Stitch	Cable Stitches

The directions for each project in this book tell you which stitch or stitches will be used; you can follow the explanations here to test each before you start a project. To create one row of knitting, you almost always weave the yarn from one end of the board to the other—moving back and forth between the boards and wrapping some but not all of the needles—and then weave back to the beginning, wrapping the needles skipped the first time; this process is referred to as a *full circular*. However, there are some stitches for which you weave down the board only once, alternating from board to board and wrapping each needle as you go; this is called *consecutive weaving*. For some stitches, you'll wrap specific needles more than once before you hook over.

Once you've cast on, you can begin to weave any of the pattern stitches. Sometimes the easiest way for us to explain how to weave the yarn is to identify the needles in sequence by number, so you can count to find which one to wrap. When we refer to *needle #1* or *the first needle*, we mean the first needle with a stitch at the left (or right) end of the board—which end is always specified. *Needle #2* refers to the needle to the right (or left) of needle #1—the next needle inside the knitted area—and so on. The knitting doesn't always start at the outside edge of the board, and you'll see empty needles there—don't count those!

To test the pattern stitches, cast on an even number of stitches; work with at least twelve stitches so you can see the results and measure the gauge (see page 17).

Stockinette Stitch

This is the most basic stitch in all knitting; perfect for beginners as well as being beautiful for nearly anything you want to make. It creates a nice smooth fabric with uniform vertical ribs. In conventional two-needle knitting, it is made by repeating a *knit* stitch across the front of the fabric and a *purl* stitch across the back. Stockinette is the best stitch to use with mohair, bouclé, or fancy designer yarns with a lot of hairs or dangly filaments, because these yarns create plenty of interest on their own and tend to obscure complex stitches. For clarity, we've used a contrasting yarn to demonstrate this technique.

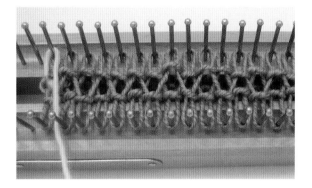

To begin, cast on using the method indicated in your project directions or any method you prefer. Position the board so the working yarn is coming from the first needle at the left end of the front board. Wrapping from the outside (as if the white yarn were a continuation of the green), pass the yarn up and around the first needle on the back board.

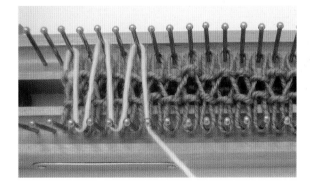

Weave the yarn down, around needle #2 on the front board (skipping the needle directly opposite your starting needle), and then back up and around needle #3 on the back board. Then weave down and around needle #4 on the front board and up around needle #5 on the back board.

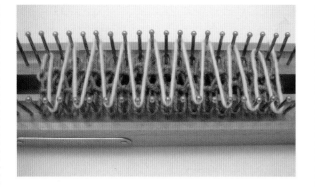

Continue to weave back and forth, around the outside of every other needle on each board. When you reach the end, wrap the last needle on the front board and pass the yarn straight back.

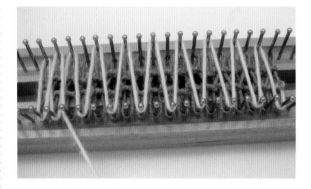

Turn the board around. Repeat the process back to the beginning, this time weaving around the needles skipped the first time.

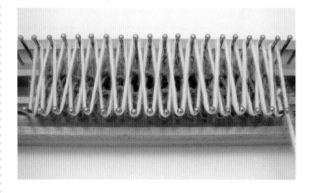

End the weaving at the needle directly across from the loop knot. This completes one full circular of Stockinette Stitch. To continue, hook over all needles and then repeat the process.

Purl Stitch

This is another basic stitch. Purl Stitch is actually the reverse side of Stockinette in conventional two-needle knitting, with horizontal loops appearing in rows across the work. When you work Stockinette Stitch in double knitting, the purled side of the fabric doesn't show because the back of the knit stitches on one layer faces the back of the other layer—the Purls are between the boards. On a knitting board, you can purl both faces of the fabric. You can also work Purl Stitch across one board and Stockinette Stitch across the other board, so your double-knit fabric looks more like conventional single knitting.

Additionally, you can intersperse Purl Stitch with Stockinette Stitch on the knitting board just as you can in two-needle knitting—the contrast of Knit and Purl creates a texture and is the basic way to make a design in the fabric without changing yarn color. If you are creating a design or motif with the Purl Stitch, you may want to work from a graph as you would for a multicolor pattern, which we'll get to later; see Charted Designs (page 52).

Purling is a variation on Stockinette Stitch (page 27), so make sure you understand that technique before you practice this one. For clarity, we've used a contrasting yarn to demonstrate.

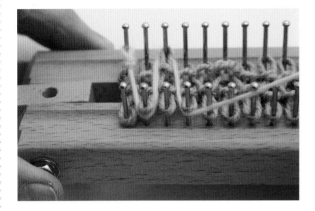

The sequence of weaving from one needle to the next is the same for purling as for Stockinette, but instead of placing each wrap on top of the existing loop on the needle, you place it below: For every stitch you want to purl on each board, weave the yarn below the existing loop on that particular needle —so the new loop lies between the existing loop and the board. You may need to use your other hand to lift the original loop up so the new loop fits next to the board. If you want to Purl just one side of the fabric, wrap the lower weave on only that side of the board. If you want both sides to look alike, wrap the lower weave on the corresponding pair of needles on both boards.

All the stitches on the front board are wrapped for Purling, with the loops of the new row (white yarn) lying between the loops of the previous row (green yarn) and the board.

You may find it easier to use a crochet hook rather than a knitting hook to lift Purl Stitches over the needles. Insert the crochet hook down into both loops from the top (insert the hook next to the needle).

Catch the lower loop (the new loop; in white yarn here) and lift it up through the original loop.

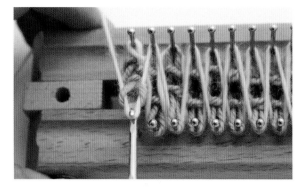

Lift the new loop off the needle. With your other hand, push the original loop up and off the needle as well, so it drops over the new loop.

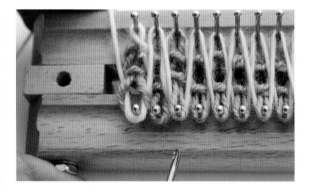

Then place the new loop back onto the needle.

Hook the rest of the Purl Stitches in the same way. If you are working a pattern in which some of the stitches on the board are wrapped for Stockinette Stitch, hook over all the Purl Stitches first and then hook over the Stockinette Stitches in the usual manner. To continue, turn the board around and repeat the process.

Rib Stitch

Rib Stitch gives knitting an elastic quality—it stretches but will snap back to its original size. Cuffs, hems, and turtlenecks are just some of the places where you may wish to use Rib Stitch, so you can see why it's an essential stitch to learn. You must cast on an even number of stitches for Rib Stitch. Every two stitches form one rib; sometimes we refer to this as a *Two-Stitch Rib*. (If you are familiar with conventional two-needle knitting, this Rib Stitch is different; it does not alternate Knit and Purl stitches.) It is worked similarly to Stockinette Stitch (page 27), with just a small change. For clarity, we've used a contrasting yarn to demonstrate.

To begin, cast on using the method indicated in your project directions or any method you prefer. Position the board so the working yarn is coming from the end needle on the left on the front board (as if the white yarn were a continuation of the red yarn in the following photos).

Wrapping from the outside, pass the yarn up and around the first needle on the back board. Weave the yarn down, around the third needle from the left on the front board, and then back up and around the third needle on the back board. Next, bring the yarn forward, skipping the fourth needle, and wrap it around the fifth needle on the front board; pass it back and wrap the fifth needle on the back board.

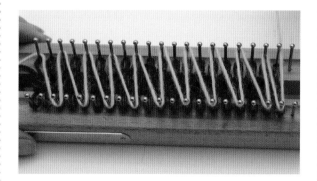

Continue to weave back and forth, around the outside of every other needle on each board. You can see that the weave crosses the board at an angle. Continue until you've wrapped one less needle on both boards than the total required. For the last stitch, wrap the next needle on the front board instead of skipping one— the last two stitches are on consecutive needles.

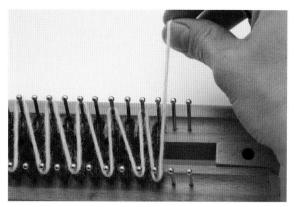

Pass the yarn back, straight across the end of the board.

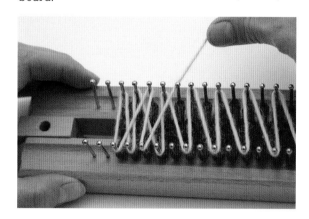

Turn the board around and repeat the process, this time weaving around the needles skipped the first time.

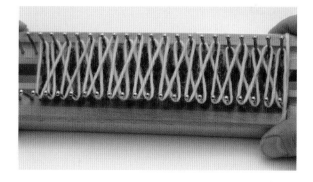

When you reach the end (where you began the ribbing), the last two wraps on the back board will be on consecutive needles. This completes one full circular in Rib Stitch. To continue, hook over all the needles and then repeat the process.

Open Rib Stitch

The Open Rib is a nice chunky version of the traditional Rib Stitch. The two sides are different: The front is chunky, as shown in the photo on page 30, and the back is the regular Rib Stitch seen in the photo above. You must use an even number of stitches for Open Ribbing.

To begin, cast on using the method indicated in your project directions or any method you prefer. Position the board so the working yarn is coming from the left end of the front board.

To set up the chunky side of the Open Rib, move the loop at the left end of the front board to its right, placing it onto the second needle. Then move the third loop onto the fourth needle.

Continue across the front board in this manner, moving every other loop onto the needle to its right, so that every other needle on that side of the board has two loops and the ones between are empty. Leave the stitches on the back board as they are, one loop on each needle. The stitches are now ready to weave in Open Rib Stitch.

For clarity, we've used a contrasting yarn to demonstrate the weaving sequence. Start at the left end (as if the white yarn in the photo were the continuation of the red) and weave the yarn back and forth around every other needle on each board, as shown, wrapping first around a needle with two loops on the front board and then around its opposite needle on the back board. In other words, the empty needles remain empty and the back board is worked with every other needle.

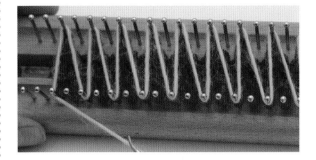

Continue across the board this way. When you get to the end of the row, turn the board around and bring the working yarn forward, straight across the board, holding it on the outside of the left needle on the front board. The chunky side of the pattern is now on the back board.

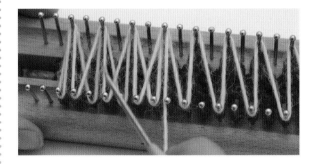

Pass the yarn around the left needle on the front board and then, wrapping on the outside, around the first needle on the back board. Now weave the yarn back and forth around every other needle on each board, as shown, wrapping around the needles previously wrapped on the chunky side and the ones previously skipped on the other side.

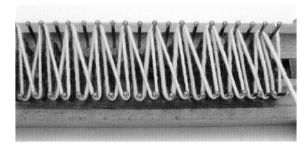

This is how the finished weaving looks from above, with the chunky side of the Rib on the back board. Each needle on the front board has two wraps.

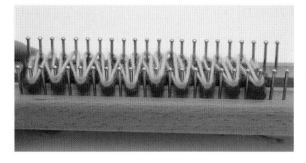

If you turn your board, this is how the weaving looks on the chunky side. The end needles and every other needle between them have four wraps each; the alternate needles are empty.

To hook over the chunky side, lift the two bottom loops on each needle up and over, leaving the two top loops on each needle.

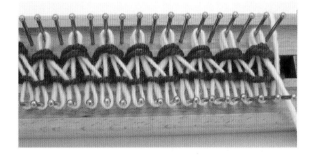

On the opposite side of the board, hook over as usual, so that each needle has one loop. This completes one row of Open Rib Stitch. To continue, position the board so the chunky side is in front again, and repeat the weaving-and-hooking process.

Open Braid Stitch

The Open Braid Stitch is a lacy ribbed design. It is a very pretty choice for afghans and baby blankets. For clarity, we've used a contrasting yarn to demonstrate this technique.

To begin, cast on using the method indicated in your project directions or any method you prefer. Position the board so the working yarn is coming from the left end of the front board.

Start at the left end (as if the white yarn in the photo were the continuation of the blue). Wrap the yarn from the outside around the first needle on the back board, next around the fourth needle on the front board, and then around the third needle on the back board. Bring the yarn forward to wrap needle #6 on the front board.

Patterns:
Mystic shawl 144

Continue weaving the yarn back and forth around every other needle on each board as shown. When you reach the end, wrap the last needle on the front board and pass the yarn straight back.

Turn the board around. To return to the other end, wrap all the empty needles as follows: needle #1 on the front board, then needle #2 on the back board, and then needle #2 on the front board. Next wrap needle #4 on the back board and then needle #3 on the front board. Continue weaving the yarn back and forth around every other needle on each board, as shown.

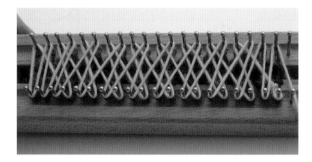

When you reach the end (where you began the Open Braid), the last three wraps will be on consecutive needles as shown. This completes one full circular in Open Braid. To continue, hook over all the needles and then repeat the process.

Double Rib Stitch

If you like the effect of Rib Stitch and Open Braid Stitch, this nice variation is similar but with a wider rib; it looks best worked with a minimum of twelve stitches. For clarity, we've used a contrasting yarn to demonstrate this technique. To begin, cast on an even number of stitches using the method indicated in your project directions or any method you prefer (we don't recommend casting on in Double Rib Stitch). Position the board so the working yarn is coming from the left end of the front board.

Start at the left end (as if the white yarn were the continuation of the blue). Wrap the yarn from the outside around the first needle on the back board and then around the third needle on the front board. Next, wrap needle #2 on the back board and then needle #4 on the front board. Then wrap needle #5 on the back board (skipping needles #3 and #4). Next, wrap needle #7 on the front board (skipping needles #5 and #6). Pass the yarn back and wrap needle #6 on the back board, then pass it forward and wrap needle #8 on the front board. Continue to weave back and forth across the board, wrapping two needles and skipping two needles on each as shown. When you reach the end, wrap the last needle on the front board and pass the yarn straight back.

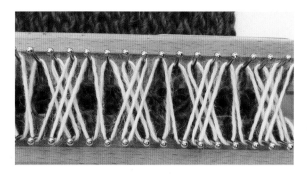

Turn the board around. To return to the other end, wrap the first needle on the front board and then weave back and forth to wrap each empty needle in turn.

Loopy Rib Stitch

The Loopy Rib Stitch is soft and open. It is a great stitch for shawls, scarves, and afghans. It also makes beautiful baby blankets and accessories. The Loopy Rib Stitch must be cast on by wrapping large loops around two adjacent needles (it can't be worked over any of the other cast-on methods), and it creates a lovely loose edge. For every stitch you want, you need two needles on each board; in other words, if your project directs you to cast on twenty stitches, you need forty needles on each board. The sample shows eleven stitches cast on over twenty-two needles on each board.

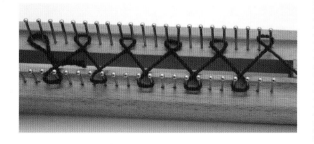

To begin, make a large loop knot (page 21) and place it over needles #1 and #2 on the back board. Pass the yarn forward to the right of needle #4 on the front board; wrap clockwise around needles #4 and #3 on the front board. Pass the yarn back to the right of needle #6 on the back board; wrap counterclockwise around needles #6 and #5 on the back board. Continue in this way to weave back and forth across the board, skipping two needles and then wrapping the next two with one loop. If you're working on an odd number of stitches, the final loop you need falls on the back board; in this case, wrap the yarn counterclockwise, as shown. If you're working on an even number of stitches, your final loop falls on the front board; in this case, wrap the yarn clockwise.

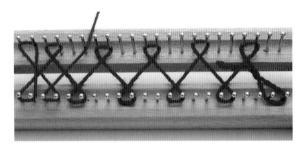

Turn the board around. Pass the yarn from the last loop made (now the first loop at the left end of the board) straight across the board, so it passes between the second and third needles on both boards. Wrap the yarn around needles #1 and #2 on the board where those needles are empty (which board depends on whether you are working with an odd or even number of stitches), and then weave back and forth across the board to wrap the sets of empty needles in sequence, wrapping clockwise on the front board and counterclockwise on the back board as before. You can see an *X* form where the yarn crosses the open space between the boards.

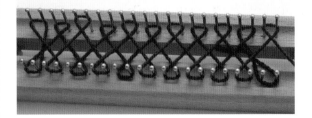

Continue wrapping until each set of needles has a loop. This completes one full circular in Loopy Rib. Keep tension on the working yarn.

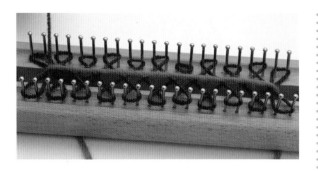

Turn the board around. Lay an anchor yarn over the weaving (see Cast On with Anchor Yarn, page 21).

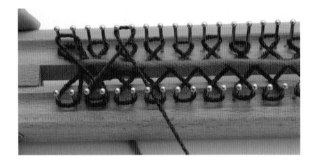

Starting at the left end of the back board, repeat the weaving pattern to make another loop on top of every other existing loop.

When you reach the end, turn the board around and weave a loop on top of the loops you just skipped, to complete another full circular, as shown. To continue, hook over all the stitches, lifting each bottom loop up and over both the needles it wraps. Pull down on the anchor yarn. To knit the Loopy Rib fabric, wrap another full circular and hook over; repeat until your work is the desired length.

tip:

You cannot bind off in Loopy Rib Stitch to match the cast-on, so if you wish to make something with the same loose effect on both ends, you should make it in two pieces—each half the total desired length. Bind off each one using the Soft Crochet (Two-Loop) Bind-Off (page 64) and then sew the bound-off edges together. You may also use the Bind Off in Pattern method (page 65) using Rib Stitch.

Zigzag Stitch

The Zigzag Stitch is our original border stitch. It makes a beautiful cuff or border on afghans and sweaters, and can also be used for the edges of scarves and hats. Instead of a full circular, Zigzag Stitch requires only a single pass down the board; for each subsequent row, turn the board around and then repeat the weaving process. This is one stitch where the weaving on the front and back boards is not identical, so don't worry that it should be. For clarity, we've used a contrasting yarn to demonstrate this technique.

To begin, cast on using the method indicated in your project directions or any method you prefer. Position the board so the working yarn is coming from the needle at the left end of the front board (as if the white yarn were a continuation of the blue yarn). Follow the photos to see how the yarn makes a complete wrap around the needle where the weaving changes direction.

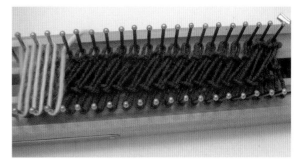

To begin, weave the yarn around needle #1 on the back board and then needle #1 on the front board. Then weave back and forth across the board to wrap needle #2 and then needle #3 on each board.

Pass the yarn from needle #3 on the front board back to the outside of needle #1 on the back board.

Wrap around needle #1 and then around needle #4 on the front board. Next, wrap around needle #2 on the back board and then needle #5 on the front board. Continue to weave the yarn back and forth at this angle across the board, wrapping around each needle in turn.

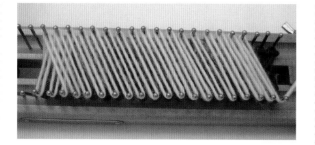

Continue until all the needles on the front board are wrapped; the last three needles on the back board should not be wrapped (they have one loop from the previous row).

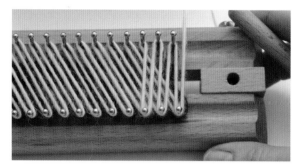

Counting from the right end of the board, pass the yarn back and around needle #3 on the back board and then around needle #3 on the front board. Then weave back and forth across the board to wrap needle #2 and then #1 on each board.

For the first row after the cast-on: Note that at each end of the board there are three loops on each of the three end needles with the overlap wrap on one side of board but only two loops on each of the other needles. The working yarn is at the end opposite the beginning of the Zigzag weave. *For all subsequent rows:* There are three loops on each of the three end needles—those with the overlap and those without, as shown in the photo at top right, and two loops on each of the other needles.

For the first row after the cast-on: To hook over, lift the bottom loop on each needle and pass it up and over the needle; where there are three loops in the overlap areas, leave the top two on the needle. All other needles will have one loop as usual after you hook over.

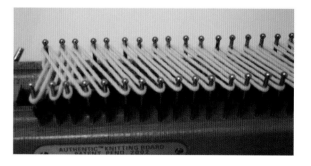

For all subsequent rows: Hook over as follows—for the three needles at each end *with* overlap, lift one over two; for the three needles at each end *without* overlap, lift two over one; for all other needles, lift one over one. In this manner, the end needles will always be ready for the next wrap, which will bring each back to three loops. (Don't forget, you turn the board around after hooking each row.)

Crisscross Stitch

Sometimes called a *Box Stitch*, this is a great stitch to use for an allover sweater design or for an accent mixed with smooth Stockinette. It has a lot of texture and contrast. This stitch is also perfect for items that need a rigid stitch, like bags or rugs, as it has very little stretch. The weaving pattern is the same as the Open Braid Stitch (page 34), but the point at which you start weaving for alternate rows changes, so the pattern is offset. For clarity, we've used a contrasting yarn to demonstrate this technique.

To begin, cast on using the method indicated in your project directions or any method you prefer. Position the board so the working yarn is coming from the left end of the front board. To work the Crisscross Stitch, first do a complete circular of Weave Pattern 1 and hook over and then do a complete circular of Weave Pattern 2 and hook over. Alternate the two Weave Patterns until your knitting is the desired length.

WEAVE PATTERN 1

Start at the left end (as if the white yarn were the continuation of the blue). Wrap the yarn from the outside around needle #1 on the back board, next around needle #4 on the front board, and then around needle #3 on the back board. Bring the yarn forward to wrap needle #6 on the front board. Weave back and forth across the boards, skipping every other needle.

When you reach the end, wrap the last needle on the front board and pass the yarn straight back.

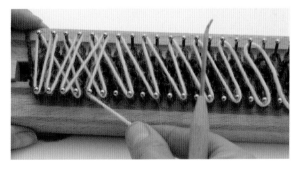

Turn the board around. To return to the other end, wrap all the empty needles as follows: needle #1 on the front board, then needle #2 on the back board, and then needle #2 on the front board. Next wrap needle #4 on the back board and then needle #3 on the front board.

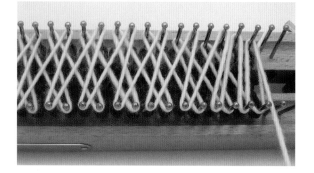

Continue weaving the yarn back and forth around every other needle on each board, as shown. Then hook over all needles.

WEAVE PATTERN 2

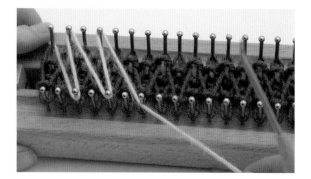

Wrap the yarn from the outside around needle #1 on the back board, next around needle #3 on the front board, and then around needle #2 on the back board. Bring the yarn forward to wrap needle #5 on the front board and then back to wrap needle #4 on the back board.

Continue weaving the yarn back and forth around every other needle on each board, as shown. When you reach the end, wrap the last needle on the front board and pass the yarn straight back.

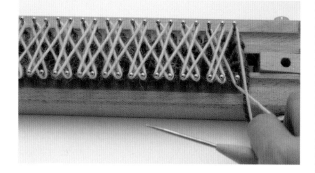

Turn the board around. To return to the beginning, wrap all the empty needles as follows: needle #1 on the front board, then needle #3 on the back board, then needle #2 on the front board. Continue weaving the yarn back and forth around every other needle on each board, as shown. To continue, hook over all needles.

Cable Stitches

Cables are formed when a few stitches on one board are lifted from their needles and transposed with the stitches adjacent to them on the same board. This crossover, called a *twist*, is worked after the weaving and hooking over of an entire row of knitting has been completed; once the stitches are transposed on the needles, they'll be secured in their new sequence by the next row of weaving. The crossover is repeated every few rows and creates a ropelike pattern that adds lots of design and texture to knitting. The stitches that are transposed are worked in Stockinette or another stitch of your choice; there is no specific weaving pattern for a cable—it's the rearranging that makes the pattern. You need two knitting hooks, crochet hooks, or cable needles (from a yarn shop) to lift and manipulate the stitches.

Cables can be interspersed with a smooth stitch like Stockinette, as shown below, with the different types of ribbing, and with other stitches, too. Most often, the cable twist is worked on just the front board and the cabled surface becomes the right side of the knitted fabric. If you are knitting something like a scarf or an afghan and would like the cable to be on both sides of the fabric, you can easily do this—just be sure to repeat the process on the back board.

Once you master the basic concept of how to twist the stitches, you can create many different and beautiful cable effects, working with different numbers of stitches to change the cable width; crossing the stitches sometimes right-over-left and other times left-over-right, which reverses the twist; and changing the number of rows between the twists (the more rows between twists, the looser and softer the cable looks). Following are two examples for you to test.

CABLES WITH STOCKINETTE STITCH

When you add cables to a Stockinette Stitch background, the cable design stands out in relief. The chunkier the yarn, the more prominent the effect. For example, let's say you want to make one large six-stitch cable down the center of a Stockinette sweater front (or swatch, if you're testing this technique).

To begin, cast on an even number of stitches using the method indicated in your project directions or any method you prefer. Find the center of the sweater front or swatch. Mark the six center needles with colored tape on the front of your knitting board. The first arm of the cable will be the three stitches to the right of center; the second arm will be the three stitches to the left of center. You can start the cable right after the cast-on or work a few rows first; on the row before you twist the cable, loosen up when you wrap and weave the six marked stitches to allow them to stretch when crossed.

Lift the loops of the three right-hand stitches off their needles and onto a knitting hook, crochet hook, or stitch holder; be sure to keep them in sequence, as shown. Then lift the loops of the three left-hand stitches onto another hook.

One at a time, transfer the loops from the right-hand hook to the three needles at the left; be sure to maintain their sequence.

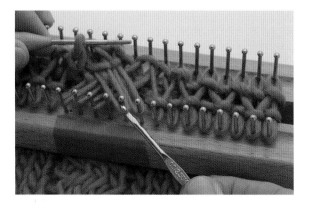

Now transfer the loops from the left-hand hook onto the three needles at the right.

Here you can see that the stitches that were on the right are now on the left. Later, when this section of your knitting emerges from between the boards, you'll see that the right arm of this cable twist crosses over the left arm on the face of your fabric.

Weave another full circular in Stockinette Stitch (shown in contrasting yarn) over the twisted loops. Hook over the row. Work a second row or more depending on the pattern repeat. Now repeat the cable twist—you can cross the stitches in the same

sequence as before or put the ones from the left onto the right-hand needles first, to change the direction of the twist. We've done some of each on this sample.

RIBBED CABLES

Cables worked in Rib Stitch are classic, and they're a favorite among knitting-board knitters because you can create so many designs—by crossing the ribs in different ways, you can "snake" the ribs over the knitted piece. One popular design features a set of four two-stitch ribs on a background of two-stitch ribs; you can see an example in the photo above. Here's what to do if you want to use this stitch on the center front of a sweater (or swatch, if you're testing this technique).

To begin, cast on an even number of stitches in Rib Stitch (page 30) and place an anchor yarn after casting on. Work at least one row in Rib Stitch. Find the center of the sweater front or swatch. Mark the eight center needles with colored tape on the front of your knitting board. This puts two ribs on each side of the center. You can start the cable right after the first Rib Stitch row or work a few more rows first; on the row before you twist the cables, loosen up when you wrap and weave the eight marked stitches to allow them to stretch when crossed.

Twist A: Begin with the four stitches on the left of your marked area. Lift the loops of the two farthest to the left off their needles and onto a crochet hook or knitting hook. Then lift the loops of the next two stitches onto another hook, as shown.

One at a time, transfer the loops from the right-hand hook to the needles on the left; be sure to maintain their sequence.

Now transfer the loops from the left-hand hook to the needles on the right.

In the same way, lift the four stitches on the right half of your marked area . . .

. . . and cross them in the same way, transferring the ones from the right-hand hook first. Here you can see that in each set of four stitches, the two stitches that were on the right are now on the left. Later, when this section of your knitting emerges from between the boards, you'll see that the right arm of this cable twist crosses over the left arm on the face of your fabric.

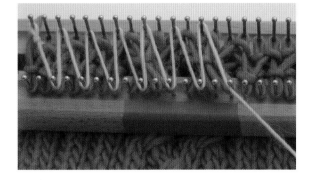

Weave another full circular in Rib Stitch (shown in contrasting yarn) over the twisted loops. Then hook over the row. Work three additional rows in Rib.

Twist B: This twist is worked on the four center stitches within the eight stitches marked and used for Twist A. Lift the two stitches to the left of center onto one hook and lift the two stitches to the right of center onto another hook, as shown.

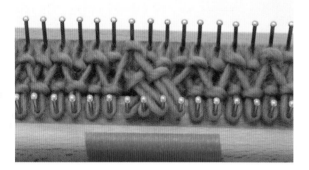

Transfer the loops from the left-hand hook to the needles on the right. Then transfer the loops on the right-hand hook to the needles on the left. (This is the opposite direction from Twist A.) To complete the pattern, work 3 rows of rib stitch after each twist. Pattern is worked as follows:

Work Twist A, work 3 rows in Rib stitch, work Twist B, work 3 rows in Rib Stitch.

Keep repeating this sequence until the piece is complete.

Let's look at another way to use ribbed cables. Create alternating blocks of cabled ribs and regular, untwisted ribs, setting up a textured checkerboard, as we did for the coat shown above. This is an effective way to use cables over the entire knitted piece rather than limiting them to one central vertical design. To do something like this, set up your piece in Rib Stitch with a multiple of 16 stitches plus 8 (to balance the pattern at the edges). Using Twist A, explained on page 43, work cables on the first eight stitches and then rib the next eight stitches. Repeat this alternating sequence of cable and rib sections across your work, then cable the last eight stitches. Continue to work Twist A and then Twist B (page 44) in the cabled sections for twelve to fifteen rows. Then switch the cable and rib sections by starting the next row with eight rib stitches followed by eight stitches in Twist A; repeat this sequence across and end with eight rib stitches. Work the patterns in this sequence for another twelve to fifteen rows, then switch the sequence again. Continue in this manner until your work is the desired length.

tip:

You can set up a checkerboard pattern with other stitch multiples, too. For instance, you could work the cables on four stitches (twisting just two two-stitch ribs) and alternate them with sections of four stitches (two two-stitch ribs) that are not twisted.

Cable Combinations

Mixing cables with other stitches can create many unique designs. Our Cabled Hat and Scarf feature bands of ribbed cables that alternate with sections of Stockinette Stitch (directions are on page 27). The scarf is made by changing the weaving patterns as you work across the knitting board. Because the knitting board creates a double-faced fabric, you can have cables on both sides of your scarf if you wish.

Creating Patterns with Color

By using yarn in a variety of colors you can create floral designs, geometric patterns, stripes, tweeds, and many other multicolor patterns with relative ease. Because the fabric is double-knit, the knots and connecting strands are hidden inside between the layers—this makes your work very neat and is one of the great things about double knitting.

It's very easy to tie on a new color, either at the beginning of a row (which puts the new color at the edge of your work) or at any point along a row: when to do this depends on the design and type of project you're creating. When you add a color, you have the option of cutting the first yarn (which makes sense if you won't need that color again soon) or leaving it attached (which enables you to pick it up again if you need only a few stitches or rows of the second color). You can continue with the stitch you've been using when you change colors. To add more interest to your knitting, you can also change to a different stitch when you change the color.

The easiest multicolor design to knit is a horizontal stripe; all you have to do is change the color for an entire row. When the designs are more complex—whether vertical stripes or something with a figured motif, like a floral or geometric shape—the yarn color must be changed at intervals across the row; this kind of knitting is called *intarsia*. It's a lot of fun, and with it your knitting can look very original and creative.

Most intarsia designs are worked following a graph, or chart, that depicts each yarn color with a different symbol or color; each square on the graph represents one stitch. When you knit, you refer to the graph, always starting at the bottom, reading just one row at a time and working the stitches in the colors indicated by the symbols. You don't need a graph for vertical stripes, because once they're set up, every row is the same. And while simple checkerboard designs don't really require a graph either—because they're a variation of vertical stripes, you just reverse the colors after working a specified number of rows—a graph may make them easier to follow.

If you enjoy intarsia knitting and want to incorporate it in an original project, remember that the gauge of your knitting (the number of stitches and rows per inch; see Check the Stitch Gauge, page 17) affects the size of the motif: A square that's 3 stitches wide and 3 rows high will be 1-inch square if your gauge is 3 stitches to the inch, but only ¾-inch square if your gauge is 4 stitches to the inch. To plan an original design, use a piece of graph paper large enough to represent the entire piece you're knitting (the front of a sweater, for instance) and draw out the entire design in color. In this chapter we explain the basics of changing color on a knitting board and demonstrate a number of intarsia patterns.

Horizontal Stripes

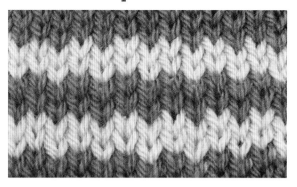

The easiest way to incorporate a multicolor pattern is by working entire rows in different colors, which creates stripes all the way across your work. For this, you may tie on the yarn at the first stitch, which puts the knot at the edge of the work (where it will show unless later hidden in a seam), or on the second or third stitch from the edge (in which case the knot will be hidden). If the knots are hidden as you work, you won't have to hide them later. So if you are making something like a scarf or an afghan where the edge will be visible, tie the yarn to the second or third stitch. Once the new and old yarns are tied together, the tails of each will lie between the front and back boards, and the next full circular row of knitting will secure them. You can work one, two, three, or more rows in the new color, or as many as you like; then work with the first color again. If you want more than two stripe colors, just tie on a third color instead of repeating the first one—you can have as many colors as you like, too.

> tip:
>
> If you know that you will be coming back to the first yarn within a few rows, you can leave it attached, tie on the new yarn and use it for as many rows as needed, then pick up the original again without having to tie it on. Be sure to lift the yarn you're not using and conceal it in the weaving as you wrap each subsequent row.

TYING ON A NEW COLOR

You can add a new color anywhere in a row. Here's the method, demonstrated at the second stitch.

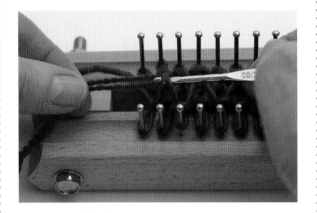

Fold a loop at the end of the new yarn. Pull it with a crochet hook under the stitch between needle #2 on the front board and needle #2 on the back board, as shown. If your stripe is to be more than a few rows, cut the first-color yarn, leaving a 2- to 3-inch-long tail. If your stripe is to be only a few rows, just pass the first color to the front of the board between the second and third needles. Then, when you weave each subsequent row, lift the yarn you are not using so that it is caught by the weaving, then pass it to the front again.

Tie the new color to the first one with a square knot.

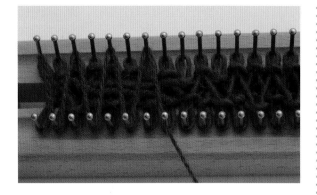

Lay the tails of both yarns on the stitches between the boards. Pass the new color back to needle #1 and weave the next row as usual.

tip:

If you are tying on a new color in order to work an intarsia design or vertical stripe, tie the new yarn to the stitch to the left of the first needle you want to be that color, between the boards—use a square knot to tie the yarn to itself around the stitch.

Vertical Stripes

Vertical stripes form perpendicular to the knitting board; they extend from bottom to top on your knitting, rather than across it like horizontal stripes. You can add a vertical stripe one to four stitches wide wherever you like, and you can have as many as you wish. Basically, you just tie on the new color where you want the stripe to begin and weave on consecutive needles instead of using a pattern stitch. To add another stripe, carry the new yarn between the boards to the next location and weave on consecutive needles again. When you've woven all the contrast stripes, go back to the beginning of the row and pick up the main color, and weave the needles you skipped when you placed the stripes, again using the pattern stitch you want for the background. Then hook over all the needles and repeat the process until the striped section of your work is as long as you wish. (If you wish to make stripes wider than four stitches, you can work them this way or use Stockinette Stitch, weaving a full circular for each section; see Weaving When the Color Changes, page 51. Consecutive weaving over more than four stitches has a slightly different tension than Stockinette and may look a little puffy.)

Here's a demonstration of how to add vertical stripes: To begin, cast on using the method indicated in your project directions or any method you like.

Before weaving either color, decide which needle you want the contrast stripe to begin on. Tie the contrast yarn to the stitch to the left of that needle, between the boards—use a square knot to tie the yarn to itself around the stitch. We're tying on at needle #4 for a stripe to begin on needle #5.

Each stripe can be anywhere from one to four stitches wide. Decide how many stitches (how many needles)

are required to make the stripe the width you want, and weave the contrast yarn around those needles consecutively. We're making this stripe two stitches wide.

If you want to make another stripe, carry the yarn to the next location and weave again; you can skip as many main-color stitches as you like between the contrast stripes. We've skipped three needles and woven two again. Repeat this process for each stripe you want. When finished, pass the contrast yarn straight across to the outside of the board, opposite the last needle woven.

Now return to the beginning end of the row and pick up the main color. Weave the pattern stitch desired for that color, skipping the needles holding the contrast stripe. (We're weaving the green yarn for Stockinette Stitch here.)

Turn the board around and complete the full circular for the first color, skipping the contrast-stripe needles again. To continue, hook over all stitches and repeat this process until the stripes are the desired length.

Checkerboards

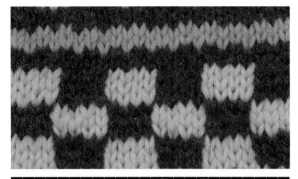

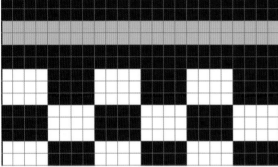

A simple checkerboard is just a variation of vertical stripes in which the colors are reversed every few rows. But if you change the proportions of the "squares" or combine them with horizontal stripes, checkerboards get a lot more interesting, as you can see in the photo above, where we used a third color to make a stripe above the slightly squat "squares." For a pattern like this, it's usually easier to keep track of the stitches if you work from a chart like the one shown below left, where each square on the grid represents one stitch. Before beginning, review Horizontal Stripes (page 47) and Vertical Stripes (page 48) as well as Weaving When the Color Changes (page 51), to be sure you understand how to tie on a new yarn and weave a row with two colors.

To begin, cast on with your main-color yarn using the method indicated in your project directions or any method you like. Make sure you have enough stitches for the Checkerboard repeat (ours is a multiple of eight stitches, four for each color).

To make our Checkerboard, work two rows in the main color (brown). Then tie on the second color (white) and weave the row, alternating four white stitches with four brown stitches, as shown on Row 3 of the chart (be sure to weave all the white stitches first, then go back to weave the brown ones). Continue to work each row as indicated on the chart—you can see that you transpose the color sequence every time you complete three rows. When the Checkerboard is complete, you can add a horizontal stripe at the top as we did.

Casting on in Vertical Stripes

You can cast on in stripes if you like. Use the Anchor Yarn Cast-On (page 21). Cast on as usual up to the point you wish the first stripe to begin, lay your main-color yarn down, and just add the new color by placing a new loop knot on the next needle. Wrap one to four stitches consecutively in the new color and then drag the yarn to additional locations as desired, wrapping each stripe on consecutive needles. Once the stripes are set, pick up the main-color yarn again and continue with the cast-on row.

WEAVING WHEN
THE COLOR CHANGES

If you are knitting broad stripes or a multicolor pattern, you have the option of weaving the main color in Stockinette Stitch while weaving the contrasting color on consecutive needles, or weaving both (or all) colors in Stockinette. Doing a broad section in consecutive weave can make the surface of your work a little puffy, so for large contrast areas that don't change shape much, it's smart to use Stockinette Stitch. But for narrower contrast areas or motifs that are irregular, it's sometimes more bother than it's worth to weave the full circular of Stockinette; we tend to use consecutive weaving in these instances. With practice, you'll see which way works for you. Here are photos showing both methods in progress for a swatch of the star motif charted on page 52.

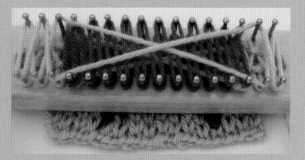

Here the full circular Stockinette is complete: You can see how the blue background yarn has been carried from one section across the contrast stitches and then worked on the second section; when the board was turned to complete the full circular, the yarn was carried across the contrast section again.

A full circular of the contrast purple yarn is woven in Stockinette Stitch before any of the blue background is worked.

The contrast purple yarn is woven consecutively prior to weaving any of the blue Stockinette Stitch background.

Here the full circular of Stockinette background is complete, and you can see how the blue yarn has been carried across the contrast section.

Charted Designs

Charted designs are graphic patterns drawn on a grid that can be worked in a variety of colors. Each square on the grid represents one stitch. To work a charted pattern, start at the bottom and work one row at a time, reading from left to right (or right to left if you weave your knitting in that way). Where can you find charted designs for the knitting board? Any design that's drawn on a grid can work; it need not be specified for the knitting board. We give some in this book, and there are many hand-knitting and needlework books with lots more that you may enjoy exploring. Here's a look at some multicolor designs that require a chart. Before deciding to use a specific design, always remember to calculate the size of the motif in the gauge of your knitting. Many designs are made of small units that are repeated over the surface of the knitting. Sometimes the unit is repeated continuously, to make an allover pattern, and sometimes it is repeated at intervals to make several isolated motifs. Refer to Weaving When the Color Changes (page 51) to see how these might look in progress.

The star and polka dots are both great examples of simple two-color motifs that are fun to work from a graph. The square-within-a-square is an easy three-color design.

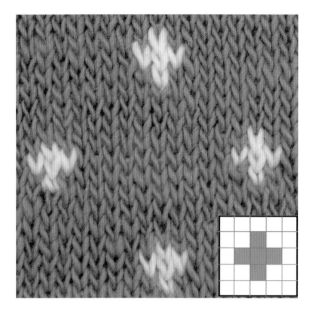

This classic fleur-de-lis motif can be repeated at whatever interval you like; it's often staggered, as shown in the photo. You can work it from a graph, but it's so easy you don't really need one: If you look at the graph, you can see that there are three stitches vertically aligned up the center of the motif; you just need to decide the interval at which to place these (the interval must be an odd number for a staggered repeat) and then work the Row 1 stitch at that interval.

This four-color design is also made of a small repeating unit. Often for designs like this, only the repeating unit would be graphed; when you knit it, you would simply work it over and over across your fabric. This pattern is used for the Rugbee Tote Bag (page 168).

This allover interlocking three-color design is actually a small square unit that is repeated continuously over the entire surface of the knitting.

This floral border design uses just three colors. It looks complicated, but since you work just one row at a time, it's quite doable. In fact, on the knitting board, this kind of motif is easy to keep track of because for each row, you weave all the stitches of a single color before weaving each of the other colors. And you weave all the stitches for a row before hooking over any of them.

Increasing and Decreasing

The processes of increasing and decreasing create variation in the shape of a knitted piece while it's on the knitting board. By adding to or reducing the number of stitches, you can change the shape from straight to flared or tapered, or from flat to rounded.

The effect varies depending on whether you make the change at the edge or at intervals across the board. When you work with a consistent number of stitches on every row, the knitting is straight—as for a scarf that's just one width for its entire length. If, instead, you want to make a sweater with a front that must be wider at the underarm, you would increase at both ends of the board so that the sides are the same; to inset the armholes, you would decrease at both ends. If you were creating a triangular shawl, you might increase on just one edge so that the work slants to one side only, and then decrease on that same edge. You frequently use increasing or decreasing to shape the brim of a hat or the shoulder of a sweater.

It's important to plan ahead for increasing when you start a project: Make sure your knitting board has enough needles for you to increase the required number of stitches to complete the piece. After you have created the additional stitches, you'll weave the next row of your work over the new loops. Once the row with the shaping has been completed, the project directions may call for you to *work straight as established* for a specified number of rows—this means to work all stitches on the board without increasing or decreasing again until directed.

tip:

The system for counting the needles adjusts along with the number of stitches when you increase or decrease. Always consider the needle at the edge of the knitting as needle #1.

Increase at the Edge

The easiest way to increase is to add a stitch right at the edge of your work. To begin, complete the row prior to the one where you wish to increase.

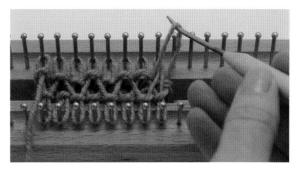

On the back board, lift the loop that was hooked over the last stitch of the previous row. Place this loop over the next empty needle.

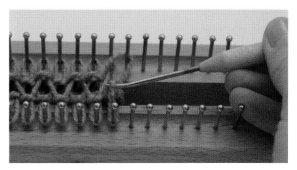

In the same way, lift the loop that was hooked over the last needle on the front board.

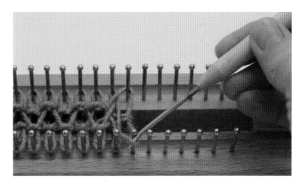

Place the lifted loop over the next empty needle. You've now increased one stitch at one end of the board. If you want to increase at the other edge of your knitting, repeat the process at the other end of both boards. Then continue your work in the established stitch.

Increase Inside

You can also make an increase one or more stitches from the edge of your work (we show one stitch from the edge here, but you can do it two or more stitches from the edge if you like). This increase creates a softer, more oval shape. To begin, complete the row prior to the one where you wish to increase.

At one end of the front board, lift the last stitch and shift it over to the next empty needle, leaving the needle it was on empty. Do the same thing with the opposite stitch on the back board. If you wish to increase at both edges, do the same thing at the other end of both boards.

Count three needles in from the end stitch on one board. Lift the previous-row loop on this needle.

Place the lifted loop over the empty needle.

Repeat this process to place a loop on each remaining empty needle. Then continue your work in the established stitch.

INCREASE ACROSS THE ROW

There are times when it makes sense to increase at intervals all across a row—for instance, for a floppy brim that you want to fan out evenly around the crown of a hat. This can easily be done in Stockinette Stitch, though it's trickier to do in many pattern stitches. Increasing at intervals across a row is done in much the same way as Increase Inside, but you must shift the stitches over from the middle of your work toward both ends of the board. If you were to repeat this process every few rows, your knit fabric would fan out considerably. In the example, we're starting with ten stitches and adding five more.

To begin, complete the row prior to the one where you wish to increase.

First, count the needles to find the middle of your work; in this case, five needles in from each end.

tip:

Move the stitches carefully, just a few needles at a time, and alternate from front board to back board so as not to stretch the yarn any more than necessary. If you are increasing a great number of stitches across a row, you may have to move each one more than once in order to place it in its final position. Get all the loops placed before you start to increase onto the empty needles. This way, you will be able to see that the placement of the increases will be balanced before filling in with the new stitches.

Starting at the left end of the back board, find the stitch to the left of the first empty needle. Lift the previous-row loop on this needle and place it over the empty needle to its right.

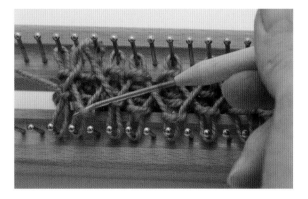

Do the same thing to the opposite stitch on the front board.

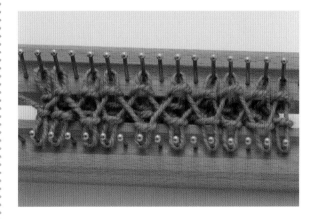

Make a plan for how to space the increases. We chose to add three stitches on one side of the middle and two stitches on the other side. Beginning at the ends, move the stitches out, in groups or singly, until you have as many empty needles as you need—one for each increase. You can see we ended up with one empty needle in the middle and two empty needles on each side of it.

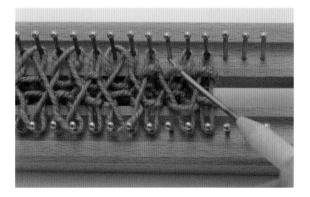

In the same way, working from both ends toward the middle, transfer a loop from the previous row onto each empty needle.

INCREASING OR DECREASING IN PATTERN STITCHES

Any time you increase or decrease, the shifting stitches will be visible. If you are working in a pattern stitch other than Stockinette, the sequence will be interrupted and the pattern will no longer work unless you plan ahead to compensate for the interruption. Increasing or decreasing in complex stitches is best handled at the edge or, if you want to do multiple increases or decreases across a row, at a point where the pattern stitch will change after the increase or decrease is worked. Every pattern stitch will be affected differently; here are some tips on how to handle three of them (if you need to increase or decrease at only one end of the row, simply work the other end in the usual manner). To begin, always complete the row prior to the one on which you wish to increase or decrease:

Rib Stitch *(page 30). Look at the Rib Stitch to see how every two stitches are pulled together to form one rib. You must increase or decrease two stitches on adjacent needles in order to add or subtract an entire rib and keep your pattern repeating evenly. You don't have to make the change all at once; here's how to do it one stitch at a time:*

Move the first and last loops at each edge over one needle to increase (or decrease). Start weaving the next row on needle #1, down to #3, then up to #2 and down to #4 rather than the usual #1 and #3. Reverse this at the end of the row. If you like, increase or decrease one stitch at each end on the next row; otherwise, repeat the adjusted sequence on each row until you are ready to add or subtract another stitch. After two stitches at each end have been added or subtracted, start on needles #1 and #3 only, as usual.

Open Braid Stitch *(page 34). Look at the Open Braid Stitch to see the stitches in ribs with yarn links between them. When you increase or decrease you must adjust the beginning of the weave to maintain the established pattern. To increase: Move the first and last loops of the row out to the next empty needle. To decrease: Move the first and last loops of the row on one needle (there will then be two loops on these needles). Then in either case, start weaving the next row on needle #1, down to needle #3, up to #2, and down to #5. Continue across, weaving every other needle; when you reach the end, reverse the sequence. Repeat the adjusted sequence on each row until you are ready to add or subtract another stitch. Then move the end stitches over one needle as before and begin weaving in the usual manner, from #1 to #4.*

Crisscross Stitch *(page 39). The two weaving patterns used for this stitch begin at different angles, causing the pattern to shift left and right on alternate rows; when you move the stitches in order to increase or decrease, you make a similar shift. Always work the first increase or decrease row after completing a row that begins with needles #1 and #4 (Weave Pattern 1). To increase: Move the first and last loops of the row out to the next empty needle. To decrease: Move the first and last loops of the row on one needle (there will then be two loops on these needles). Then, in either case, repeat Weave Pattern 1. On the next row, work Weave Pattern 2. To work straight on this number of stitches, go back to alternating the weaving patterns as before. Or if you need to decrease again, move the first and last stitches on one needle again. Repeat Weave Pattern 2. On the next row, work Weave Pattern 1. Repeat this sequence every time you need to decrease. To work straight on this number of stitches, go back to alternating the weaving patterns as before.*

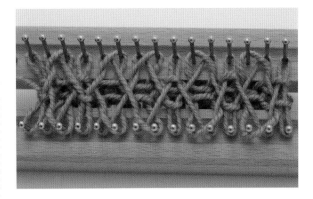

As you can see, we now have fifteen stitches on the board.

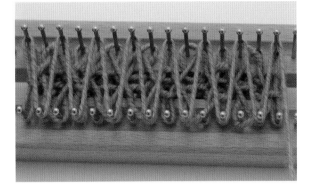

Continue your work in the established stitch, weaving around all the needles.

Decrease at the Edge

The easiest way to decrease is to remove a stitch right at the edge of your work. To begin, complete the row prior to the one where you wish to decrease.

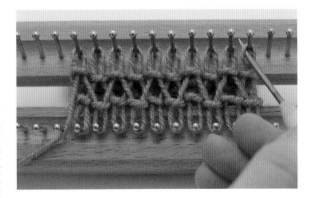

Lift the loop of the last stitch at the right end of the back board.

Place this loop onto the needle to its left (the next needle with yarn).

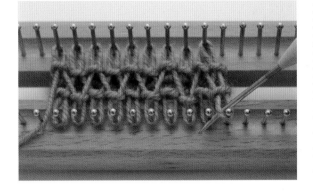

Now lift the loop on the last needle at the right end of the front board.

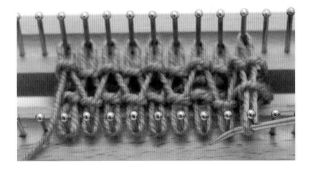

Place this loop onto the needle to its left. Now both needles at the right end of the board have two loops.

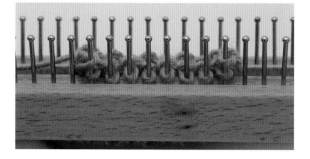

If you wish to decrease at the other end, move the stitches on the last pair of needles to their right. You can see here that there are two loops on each end needle.

Weave the yarn for the next row; there will be three loops on each end needle. When you hook over, lift both lower loops on the end needles over the top loop.

Decrease Inside

This decrease can be done anywhere in the row, near the end or elsewhere. You can repeat it at any interval (except on every stitch) across the row. To begin, complete the row prior to the one where you wish to decrease. Decide where you wish to make the decrease. In this example, we are decreasing the third stitch from the end.

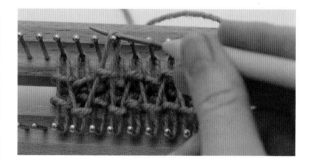

On the back board, lift the stitch you wish to decrease and move it toward the middle of the board onto the next needle.

On the front board, move the corresponding stitch toward the middle of the board onto the next needle. One pair of opposite needles is now empty.

Repeat the decrease on both boards wherever you like, being sure to move opposite pairs of stitches. If you wish to decrease at both ends of your work, shift the stitches toward the middle of the board. If you wish to decrease at intervals all the way across, shift all the stitches in the same direction. Once you have all the decreases made, move the stitches over to cover all the empty needles—start by moving the stitches closest to the middle and work out toward both ends, always moving the stitches in the same direction you did to make each decrease. You can see here that the two end stitches have been moved over and are now next to the needle with two loops, which holds the decrease.

Weave the yarn for the next row; there will be three loops on each decrease needle. When you hook over, lift both lower loops on the decrease needles over the top loop.

INCREASE WITH AN EYELET

You may want to incorporate a decorative Eyelet Stitch in the increase row, which looks pretty across a sweater or at a neckline. An Eyelet Increase is usually incorporated in Stockinette Stitch knitting or worked at a point in the project where the pattern stitch is about to change. Say, for example, you are making a Stockinette Stitch sweater and you want to increase at the neckline to create a floppy collar. You could use the Eyelet Increase and then work the collar in another stitch if you like. Or do the reverse: Make the sweater in Crisscross, increase with Eyelet, and change to Stockinette for the collar. This technique is begun similarly to Increase Across the Row (page 56), but you don't transfer loops from the previous row to the empty (increase) needles. In this example, we're starting with nine stitches and adding four more. To begin, complete the row prior to the one where you wish to increase.

Weave the next circuit of loops onto all the needles. You can see here that the needles that were empty (the increase stitches) now have one loop, and the other needles have two loops.

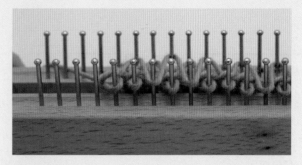

Hook over all needles except the increase stitches, which have only one loop.

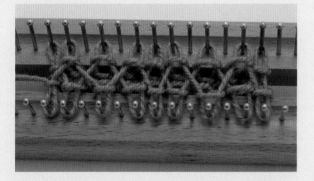

Each eyelet requires one pair of opposite needles on the board. Decide on an interval for the eyelets—we've chosen a varied interval of one or three stitches. Beginning at the ends of the board, move the stitches out—in triplets, pairs, or singly—until you have as many empty needles as you need. Do not lift any prior-row loops onto the empty needles.

Weave all needles again, so there are two loops on each, and hook over all the stitches. Then continue your work in the established stitch. After a few rows, you'll see the increase stitch with the eyelet below it.

Binding Off

Binding off is the process of removing your knitted fabric from the knitting board in a way that secures the stitches so your work won't unravel. There are a couple of ways to do this: *Bind Off with Crochet Chain*, which gives a very stable edge; and *Bind Off in Pattern*, which is more elastic. Most project directions will indicate which method to use. Additionally, if you have cast on using an anchor yarn (page 21), you'll often want to finish the cast-on edge and remove the anchor. The process for this is similar to binding off from the board, so it is explained at the end of this section (page 66).

Bind Off with Crochet Chain

This bind-off method creates an even Chain Stitch along the edge. It has very little stretch and looks very uniform and finished. You can use a crochet hook or your knitting hook to do it. There are two variations on this technique: The first gives a tight, firm edge; the second produces a slightly softer, looser edge.

FIRM CROCHET (THREE-LOOP) BIND-OFF

Start at the end of the board opposite the working yarn. You may cut the excess yarn before binding off, but be sure to leave a 3- to 4-inch-long tail.

With a crochet hook, lift the first loop on the front board off its needle, and then lift off the first loop on the back board.

Lift off the next loop on the front board. You have three loops on the crochet hook.

Partial Row Bind-Off

There are times when you need to bind off from both edges of the knitting but leave the center stitches on the board for further work. For instance, on a sweater you sometimes slant the shoulders from the armhole edge toward the back neck. In order to keep the working yarn available for the remaining stitches when you do this, work as follows:

Bind off from the right edge as indicated in your project directions (or the edge opposite the working yarn); transfer the last loop onto the next needle to the left on one board. Then lift the working yarn from the left edge and lay it between the boards, across the number of stitches to be bound off. Now bind off from the left edge and place the last loop on the next needle to the right on one board. Pick up the working yarn and continue to work the remaining stitches as instructed. Note that the end needles on one board now have two loops; be sure to lift both these loops when you hook over the next row.

Using your other hand for assistance, pull the loop closest to the hook through the other two loops. There is one loop left on the hook.

Lift off the next loop on the back board, and then the next one on the front board. Again, there are three loops on the crochet hook. Pull the loop closest to the hook through the other two loops.

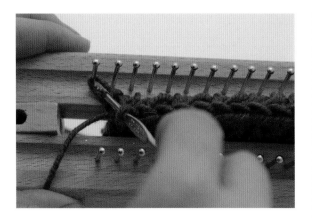

Continue the process across the board. You may end with only two loops on the hook. If so, just pull the loop closest to the hook through the other, ending with one loop remaining on the hook.

Cut the excess yarn if you haven't already done so. Pull the yarn tail through the loop on the hook, forming a knot.

Pull the tail of yarn between the knitted layers for a nice finish.

SOFT CROCHET (TWO-LOOP) BIND-OFF
If you want the edge to be a bit softer, try this version:

Work this method as you did the firm method, but lift off just two loops—first one from the front board and then one from the back board—and pull the one closest to the hook through the other.

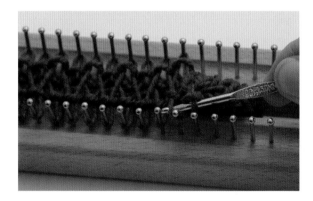

Continue lifting off one loop from the front board and pulling it through the loop already on the hook.

Continue this process, lifting one loop at a time from alternate boards, until you come to the end and have only one loop remaining on the hook. Pull the yarn tail through the last loop, forming a knot, and tuck the tail between the knitted layers.

Bind Off in Pattern

Use this technique when you want the edge of the knitting to stretch and look like part of the pattern stitch. You can use it with the Rib or Open Rib Stitches (shown in the bottom photo on page 66), Open Braid and also the Zigzag Stitches (pages 30, 32, 34, and 37, respectively). Start at the end of the board opposite the working yarn. Use a crochet hook to manipulate the stitches.

Look at the weave completed on the board. You will see the loops that belong in the same Rib or Braid. You'll keep the loops of each group together as you bind off.

To begin, reduce the number of loops of the first group on one board. Lift off the first two loops and pull the one closest to the hook through the other one. (If there is a third loop, which may occur right at the edge of your work, as in the photo, lift it off and pull it through the other loop on the hook). When only one loop remains in the group, put it back on a needle.

Work across the board to reduce the number of loops in each group to one. Then do the same on the other board. When you've finished, you'll have a loop on every other needle. Make sure the loops don't jump off the needles. If you look at the knitting from under the side of the board, you will see that the Rib or Braid Stitch is still defined.

To bind off, begin again at the end opposite the working yarn. Lift the first loop on the front board off its needle, and then lift off the first loop on the back board. Pull the loop closest to the hook through the other loop. Then lift off the next loop on the front board and pull it through the other loop on the hook.

Continue the process across the board, lifting one loop at a time from alternate boards, until you come to the end and have only one loop remaining on the hook. Pull the yarn tail through the last loop, forming a knot, and tuck the tail between the knitted layers. See how the bound-off edge has the Rib or Braid or Zigzag effect of the pattern stitch.

This is what the Open Rib Stitch looks like when bound off in pattern. This same process can be done with any stitch, and if you have a series of stitches you can vary the groups on the front and back boards to match the stitch. For example, if you are doing the Zigzag Stitch (page 37), you would want to alternate every other stitch on the front and back boards to get an effect of continuing the Zigzag.

Bind Off to Remove the Anchor Yarn

If you begin your work by casting on over an anchor yarn, the cast-on edge remains loose unless you do something to secure it. For some projects, say the top of a hat, you'll actually gather the stitches by pulling the anchor yarn tight. But if you want the edge to be flat and firm, you can use a crochet hook to "bind off" the stitches, much as you would if they were on the needles of the knitting board. This can be done working with three loops at a time or just two, for a looser edge. The photos show the three-loop version.

Hold the knitting in your left hand, with the loop knot and working yarn at the left end. Insert the crochet hook into the first three loops at the right end of the knitting (the gray yarn tail in the photo is the anchor yarn).

Pull the loop closest to the hook through the other two loops.

There is one loop left on the hook.

Insert the hook through the next two loops. Pull the loop closest to the hook through the other two. Continue this process across the knitted piece. You may end with only two loops on the hook. If so, just pull the loop closest to the hook through the other, ending with one loop remaining on the hook.

Cut the excess yarn if you haven't already done so. Catch it with the hook.

Pull the yarn tail through the loop on the hook, forming a knot. Then pull the tail of yarn between the knitted layers for a nice finish. Carefully pull out the anchor yarn.

The finished cast-on edge looks smooth, rimmed with even Chain Stitches.

tip:

If you are making a scarf or similar item where both ends should be the same, always mimic the stitch sequence used to remove the piece from the board when you bind off to remove the anchor yarn. Or place the stitches back on the needles and bind off just as you did to remove the other end of the piece from the board.

Plackets, Buttonholes, and Pockets

Simple pullover sweaters are great, but what if you'd like a cardigan with buttons and buttonholes? You can add a placket band to give the overlapping edges a stable, attractive finish. And how about a place to warm your hands or put some change? You can choose between super-easy patch pockets or slash pockets, which are a bit more involved but not as bulky.

Placket Band

A placket band is an extra-thick section, several stitches wide, along the vertical edge of the knitted fabric; it helps retain the shape and reduces the amount of stretch in that area. It's usually worked in Stockinette Stitch (page 27) and created by weaving an additional full circular of the desired number of stitches along the edge. A placket band can be worked at either or both ends of the knitting board. It is ideal for the front edge of a sweater or coat, especially to support buttonholes and buttons, or for anywhere you'd like to reinforce a vertical edge, like a sleeve vent. If you like, work the placket band in a contrasting color, as if you were making a vertical stripe (page 48)—the band of color can be great on a jacket or a blanket. Placket bands can also be worked anywhere there is a vertical opening, such as a neckline, pocket slit, or sleeve vent; for how to do this, read Slash-Pocket Placket Bands (page 75).

Placket bands are most often worked on four to eight stitches at the edge of the knitted fabric. You can begin or end a placket band at any point along the length of your work, but—with the exception of a side seam vent—they're most commonly used along the entire edge of a piece. To begin, cast on using the method indicated in your project or whichever method you prefer. Decide how wide you want the reinforced area to be and, as explained in this section, work the placket band on the number of stitches needed to create that width (see Gauge, page 17). The following photos show the placket band already in progress, worked on six stitches at the left end of the board. See the Tip at the end of this section to make a placket at the right end of the board.

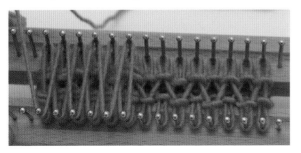

When you begin the row, using Stockinette Stitch, weave only the number of stitches needed for the desired placket-band width. Then turn the board

around and complete the circular back to the beginning of the row. Do not hook over the stitches at this point. If this is the first row after the cast-on, there will be three loops on each placket-band needle; all subsequent rows will have four loops on each needle.

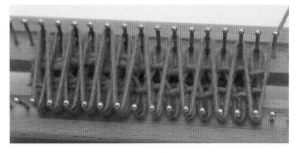

Now weave in Stockinette Stitch across the entire row—over the placket-band stitches again and then all the rest of the stitches.

Turn the board around and complete the full circular on the entire row. The placket-band needles (now at the right end of the board) have four loops and the other needles have two loops.

Hook over the stitches; For the placket-band stitches, lift the two lower loops over the needle and hook the remaining stitches as usual. There will be two loops on each placket-band needle and one loop on the others. (If this is the first row after the cast-on, hook over one loop in the placket-band area, leaving two loops on each placket-band needle.)

Repeat this process on every row until the placket band is the desired length.

To make a placet at the right end

tip:

To make a placket at the right end of the board, weave from left to right as usual. Then work a full circular (right to left, left to right) on the number of stitches desired for your placket. Then weave a complete row from right to left and hook over as explained in this section.

Buttonholes

There are many situations when you may want to include a button fastening in your project. Up the front of a sweater or coat, say, or at the top of a bag or the edge of a shawl. Garments often have a reinforced edge called a placket band (page 68), which makes a great support for buttonholes and buttons, but bags, shawls, and other items may not. It doesn't matter whether you have a placket band or not—buttonholes can be incorporated in either case. They're worked into the fabric as you knit: To make them, you temporarily move a loop from one needle to its neighbor to create a hole. The method is a little different depending on whether you've got a placket band or not. The size of the buttonhole depends to some extent on the yarn and board you are using, so it's smart to make a test or buy the buttons after you've made the buttonholes. If you wish to use a large button, see Making a Larger Buttonhole or Making a Button Loop on page 72.

BUTTONHOLE IN PLACKET BAND

Use this method if you are making a narrow band that is only a few stitches wide. Place the buttonhole as close to the middle of the placket band as you can, but allow at least two stitches (two needles) from the edge of the work to the one used for the buttonhole. For example, if you are making a baby sweater that has a narrow, four-stitch placket band, work the buttonhole on needle #3. In the example shown here, the placket band is six stitches wide and the buttonhole is worked on needle #4. Remember, the needles for the placket-band stitches have two loops each (at the left end of the work, in these photos) and the other needles have one loop each. To begin, weave and hook over the row where you wish to make the buttonhole, including the placket band, as usual.

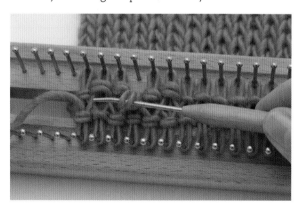

On the back board, lift the loops off needle #4.

Using your fingers as shown, transfer one loop to needle #3 and the other to needle #5 on the same board, leaving needle #4 empty.

Now, on the front board, lift the loops off needle #4.

Transfer one loop to needle #3 and the other to needle #5 on the same board. Needle #4 on both boards is now empty.

To continue, weave the next row, including the placket band, as usual. There will be only two loops on needle #4. Hook over the row, omitting needle #4. Weave another row, including the placket band. Now there are four loops on each placket-band needle. Hook over the entire row as usual.

tip:

To plan the spacing of buttonholes for a garment, knit the piece to which you want to sew the buttons first. That way you can arrange the buttons on it at the interval you like, mark each placement, and then count the rows between the markers to see how often to work a buttonhole on the corresponding piece.

BUTTONHOLE WITHOUT PLACKET BAND

In Crisscross Stitch

Use this method to work one or more buttonholes across a row of knitting; however, if your row contains only a few stitches, use the Buttonhole in Placket Band method (page 70). You can make this buttonhole anywhere in the row; it can be completed using any stitch (there are several examples shown above, below, and on page 72) and doesn't change the weave pattern. Once you choose where to work it, just manipulate the stitches as explained in this section. To begin, weave and hook over the row where you wish to make the buttonhole. Decide which needle will be the buttonhole.

In Rib Stitch

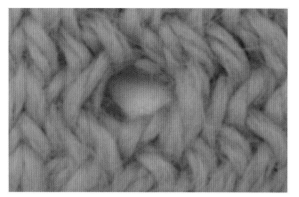

In Zig Zag Stitch

On the front board, lift the loop off the needle where you wish to make the buttonhole and, moving it away from the project edge, transfer it to the adjacent needle (so there are two loops on that needle). Do the same on the back board, being sure to move the loop in the same direction.

To continue, weave the next row as usual. There will be one loop on the buttonhole needle (the one that was empty) and three loops on the one that had two loops. Hook over the row, omitting the needle with one loop and lifting the two bottom loops over the top on the needle that has three loops. Weave another row. Now there are two loops on every needle, and you can hook over as usual.

Making a Larger Buttonhole

You can make a much larger and nicely shaped buttonhole if you temporarily move the stitches off two needles instead of just one: Choose the location of the buttonhole and identify the two stitches on each board. Lift each stitch and place it on the adjacent needle (moving one to the left and one to the right). Weave the next row over the empty needles, creating a single loop on both. When you hook over the row, do nothing to these two needles. Weave the next row (there will be two stitches on each needle) and proceed with the knitting as usual. If you do this with the Rib Stitch, be sure to place the buttonhole on one rib.

Making a Button Loop

Button loops are a fine alternative to button-holes. They work well when the knitted fabric is very thick, or the button you want to use is very large; you may just like the way they look. Also they're added when the knitting is complete, so you don't have to plan ahead for them. A button loop is simply a crocheted chain of yarn, just like a short Drawstring (page 83). Make each loop four times the button diameter, or the length indicated in your project directions. Overlap the pieces of the project to align as you wish. Sew on the buttons. Fold each button loop and slip it around a button; pull the ends of the loop into the knitting, making sure you can slide the button through the loop. Then knot the ends of the loop or secure them in a seam, as appropriate for your piece, and secure them with a few stitches if needed. (Instead of extending the loops from the edge of the knitting, you can position them flush against the edge if you prefer; experiment to see which shape secures your pieces best.)

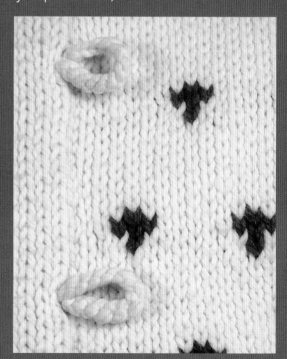

SEWING ON BUTTONS

When sewing a button to double-knit fabric, it is important to sew loosely enough to create a little space between the button and the fabric so that, when buttoned, the thickness of the buttonhole layer will be nice and flat under the button. The amount of space to be left between the button and the knitted fabric depends on the thickness of your knitted fabric. Some buttons have a shank on their back for this purpose, but if your button is the type with holes, you'll need to create a shank by sewing loosely. We've used a contrast yarn for clarity here, but generally you'll want to use the same yarn used for the knitting or a color that matches the button. If the holes on your button are too small for a yarn needle to pass through, thread the yarn through them with a tapestry or embroidery needle (or just dampen the yarn end, compress it with your fingers, and poke it through the button).

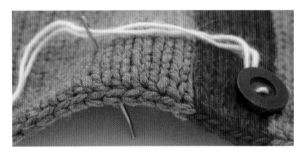

Thread the button onto a single strand of yarn about 8 to 10 inches long. Bring the yarn ends together and thread them both through a yarn needle. From the right side, insert the needle through the knitted fabric.

Pull the needle and the yarn ends through the knit fabric; gently pull the yarn until the button sits loosely above the fabric on a short shank of yarn. Pull one yarn end out of the needle, then pass the needle and the other yarn end back up the right side of the fabric. Wrap the yarn around the shank below the button several times.

tip:

Pins are likely to get lost in the knitted fabric, so try this to mark the spot where you want to sew on a button: Use a crochet hook to pull a scrap of contrasting yarn under the stitch where you want the button. There's no need to knot; it will stay in place until you pull it out.

Insert the needle back through the knitting and pull the yarn all the way through. Tie the yarn ends snugly together. Weave the ends into the knitting with a crochet hook and cut off any excess.

Pockets

Creating pockets for a double-knit garment or bag is very easy. You can knit a separate square and sew it onto the outside as a patch pocket. Or you can create a vertical opening, called a *slash*, in the knitting and then later sew a fabric or knitted pocket to the inside behind it. Pockets in knitted items aren't meant to carry heavy items, because the knitting may stretch out of shape or the sewing that secures the pocket may loosen over time.

PATCH POCKET

A patch pocket is just a square of knitting sewn to the outside of your project. You can make the patch any size you want, use any color or stitch you like and position it wherever you need it. Since you add this kind of pocket after your project is otherwise done, you don't have to worry about planning it exactly while you are knitting the main pieces. It's often nice to work a band of ribbing at the top of the pocket patch, as we did in the photo at right.

To make a patch pocket, first decide how large you want the patch to be. Then find the gauge at which you are knitting (see page 17). Multiply the width desired by the stitch gauge; the result is the number of stitches to cast on. Multiply the height desired by the row gauge; the result is the number of rows to work. For example, if your gauge is 3 stitches and 3 rows = 1 inch, and you want your pocket to be 4 inches wide and 6 tall, you would cast on 12 stitches and knit 18 rows.

When the patch is finished, pin it where you want it and sew it on with a Topstitch (page 81).

tip:

If you don't want to see the stitches securing the pocket, sew from inside the knitted piece and just pick up the back layer of the pocket rather than sewing all the way through it. When you're finished, make some reinforcement stitches at the top corners of the pocket.

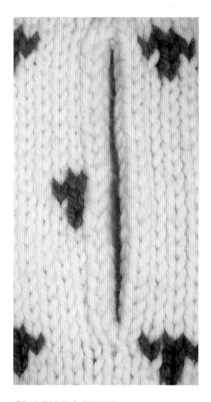

SLASH POCKET

The vertical opening for a slash pocket is usually positioned on a garment's front piece about two-thirds of the way from the center front to the side seam. You can't change your mind later about the position of the slash, so be sure to check the gauge and plan the location and length of the slash ahead of time. Once the slash is incorporated, simply finish knitting the piece as usual; you'll add the pocket lining (called a *pocket bag*) later.

The slash falls between two adjacent needles (two on the front board and the corresponding two on the back board). You work the stitches on each side of the opening with a separate ball of yarn, creating a narrow two-stitch placket band along each edge as you go (see page 68). These placket bands stabilize the slash edges and make them durable; the photo on page 74 shows a closeup view of the placket stitches at the edge of a slash.

To demonstrate how to make a slash-pocket opening, we've used contrasting yarn to show one section of the divided work. To begin, knit the piece in Stockinette Stitch (page 27) as usual up to the point where you want the bottom of the pocket opening; complete a row before starting the slash (if you want the opening to begin 10 inches above the cast-on, knit until the fabric is 10 inches long). Decide where in the width of the piece you want to locate the slash, and mark the place with a pin or a strand of yarn between those needles while you get started. In these directions *Section 1* refers to the stitches from the beginning of the row to the slash and *Section 2* refers to the stitches from the slash to the end of the row.

SLASH-POCKET PLACKET BANDS

Follow these steps to create a two-stitch placket band on each edge of the slash. Work in Stockinette Stitch. If you have not made a placket band, refer to page 68 before beginning these. It's easiest to keep track of what you're doing if you weave and hook over the first row of Section 1 before weaving and hooking over the first row of Section 2, and then continue in that way, completing one row at a time on each section in turn.

SECTION 1: *Weave from left to right to the end of Section 1; then reverse and weave the last two needles from right to left. Reverse again and weave the last two needles from left to right. Reverse once more and complete the full circular over all needles from right to left.*

On each board, the last two needles of Section 1 have three loops; hook the bottom loop over the top two loops. All the other needles have two loops; hook one over one.

Note: Section 2 is illustrated in white for clarity.

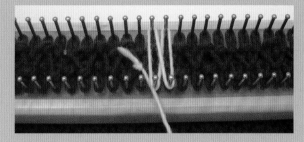

SECTION 2: *Weave the first two needles from left to right; then reverse and weave them right to left.*

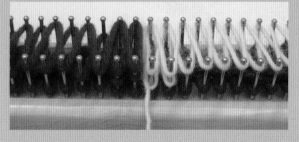

Now do a full circular over all the needles in Section 2. On each board, the first two needles of Section 2 have three loops. Hook one over two. All the other needles have two loops; hook one over one.

BOTH SECTIONS: *Continue to weave in this manner. For all subsequent rows, the last two needles of Section 1 and the first two needles of Section 2 will have four loops. On these stitches, hook the two bottom loops over the two top loops.*

Tie on a new ball of yarn where Section 2 will start (see Tying on a New Color, page 48). Transpose the stitches at the edges of the slit (see Reinforcing Weak Spots, page 30). Then begin to weave, working Section 1 from left to right up to Section 2, and then working Section 2 with the new yarn. As you do this, incorporate the placket bands as explained in Slash-Pocket Placket Bands on page 75.

Continue to knit the two sections separately, incorporating the placket band as you go, to create the opening for the pocket.

When the slash is the desired length, stop weaving the placket bands; instead, just weave one row using the yarn from Section 1 all the way across. When you get to the beginning of Section 2, cut and tie that yarn onto the yarn from Section 1. This will close the pocket opening. Hook over all needles so that only one loop remains on each. Then transpose the stitches at the edges of the slash as you did when beginning. Continue with your project.

tip:

If you don't want to create a slash in your knitting, you can simply leave a section of the side seam unsewn for the pocket opening.

When the piece is complete and off the board, you will want to create a pocket bag from warm woven or knitted fabric. Soft flannel or fleece both work well and are not bulky. The bag must be at least a little longer than the slash, and it can be considerably longer if you like. It must be wide enough to accommodate your hand.

Depending on where the pocket is and your preference, you can either make a large patch to sew behind it, as shown in the photo above, or make a two-piece bag that attaches to the slash and hangs free inside; the second is preferable if your knitted fabric is loose and open or the yarn is very soft. For the patch option, be sure to sew only to the inside layer of the knitting. For the free-hanging option, cut two pieces of fabric, one to attach to each side of the slash. Sew the two pieces together, leaving open the section that will be attached to the slash. Do not turn the bag right side out. Fold the seam allowance on the open area to the wrong side. Place the pocket bag on the inside of your project and pin the opening to the slash. Sew the bag to the slash by hand with regular sewing thread.

Finishing
Your
Projects

Ah, your knitting is complete. What's next? Finishing the piece is a fun and very important part of knitting. Done well, it gives your projects a professional look that will be truly appreciated by anyone lucky enough to receive one. You don't want to be like a great cook who prepares lots of good recipes but forgets to set a proper table, so pay as much attention to the final steps as you did to the knitting itself. Depending on what you've made, the finishing may require only trimming and tucking in yarn tails, or it may involve some sewing and adding accents like pompoms or tassels. Gather the pieces in a basket or on your table, along with all the little tools needed for doing a great finishing job (listed on page 18).

Sewing

Once the pieces of a knitted project are complete, the next step is to sew them together. Doing this neatly gives a nice professional look to hand knits. There are a number of ways to assemble the pieces; which you use depends on the project and the look you're after. Sometimes you'll want the stitching to show and other times you'll want it to be invisible or hidden. Use a yarn needle and the same-weight yarn as your project to sew; if your project is very lightweight, a tapestry needle may be used. Always insert the needle between the stitches—you don't want to split the yarn itself. Unless your yarn is very soft, sew with a single strand and don't knot the end; you'll secure the ends when you've finished all the sewing. You may wish to pin long seams before sewing. Here is an overview of the stitches you may use.

INVISIBLE STITCH

Use the invisible stitch when you want a flat, barely discernible seam. To work it, you weave the pieces together, passing the needle under the yarn strand between the layers of each piece instead of inserting it straight through the piece—this is one of the great benefits of the double-knit fabric made on a knitting board. When finished, the joined edges lie butted together instead of being layered as they are when Whipstitched (page 80) or Topstitched (page 81). Sew with the same yarn used for the knitting, in the same color. If your yarn is very soft or thin, you can sew with a double strand or make a sewing twine (page 81).

To begin, place the two pieces to be joined one on top of the other, aligning the edges you wish to sew; it doesn't matter which side of the fabric is on the outside.

Insert the sewing needle into the edge of one piece where you wish the seam to begin, sliding it under the yarn strand that links the double-faced fabric.

Pull the needle all the way through under the strand. Keeping the needle pointing in the same direction, insert it just a bit farther along the seam and slide it under a strand on the other piece.

Repeat this process, alternating from one piece to the other and moving a little bit farther along the seam with each insertion.

After you've made a few stitches, gently pull the yarn snug, but not tight, against the seam.

Continue in the same way to the end of the seam. When complete, knot the yarn at both ends or use the yarn tails to secure other pieces as your project requires. Unfold the pieces and gently press the seam with your fingers—you can see the stitches are completely hidden.

WHIPSTITCH

The Whipstitch is versatile; you'll find it works well in many project-assembly situations, especially when the edges to be joined are firm—like the selvages (side edges) of the fabric. It is very strong and does not put much stress on the stitches of the knitted fabric. It's usually worked on the wrong side (inside) of the project in the same color yarn as the knitting, but if you want to create a decorative seam you can use a contrasting yarn instead. A portion of each Whipstitch may be visible on the right side of the seam, but the yarn passes between the stitches in the same direction as the knitted yarn does and is not obvious. To begin, place the two pieces to be joined right sides together, aligning the edges you wish to sew.

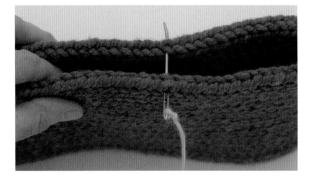

Inserting the point between the stitches where you wish the seam to begin, pass the sewing needle through one piece and then through the corresponding spot on the second piece.

Bring the needle and yarn over the top of the seam and repeat, passing them through the two pieces in the same direction.

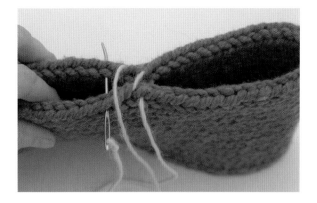

Pull the yarn snug, but not tight, over the seam. Continue in the same way to the end of the seam. When complete, knot the yarn at both ends or use the yarn tails to secure other pieces as your project requires.

tip:

Use large paper clips to secure two pieces of knitting for sewing. Uncurl the clips part way and simply slip them through the layers. You can also use small binder clips.

TOPSTITCH

The Topstitch seam is worked on the right side, or outside, of a project and forms a ridge along the project edge. The farther from the edge you sew, the larger

Sewing Twine

If the yarn you're using is fragile and frays or breaks when you sew with it, make it into a sewing twine, which will be sturdier and easier to work with. Sewing twine also works well when you want to make a very strong seam—say, for assembling a bag. To make sewing twine, cut two lengths of yarn about twice as long as you want the twine to be and tie them at one end onto a doorknob or piece of furniture. Grasp the strands loosely and stand back to put gentle tension on them, then roll them between your hands so that they twist together. Step back, keeping some tension on the strands, and adjust your hands to roll the strands together along their entire length. They will roll into a tight twine. It's easiest to sew with a 2-foot length of twine, so make short pieces or cut a longer one as you need it.

the seam ridge will be. The stitches are visible, so use a matching or contrasting yarn, as you wish.

To begin, place the two pieces to be joined wrong sides together, aligning the edges you wish to sew.

Inserting the point between the stitches where you want the seam to begin, pass the sewing needle through one piece and then through the corresponding spot on the second piece.

Pull the needle all the way through. Then insert it between stitches a short distance from where it came out and pass it through the corresponding spot on the first side.

Pull the yarn snug, but not tight, against the seam. Continue in the same way to the end of the seam. When complete, knot the yarn at both ends or use the yarn tails to secure other pieces as your project requires.

You may also use Topstitching as a decorative accent through a single layer of knitting—say, along an outside edge—or to attach a small piece like a patch pocket or pocket flap to a larger piece.

Drawstrings and Ties

Many projects call for a drawstring that can be laced through the knitted fabric to draw it up—you often need a drawstring at the top of a hat, for a hood, slippers, or at a sweater neckline. It's easy to make one by crocheting a yarn chain. You can use the same technique to make a tie, as we did to wrap the cute stack of coasters on page 91. For many projects, you may add a pompom to the ends of the strings or ties (see page 84) or even some beads.

Start with a loop knot.

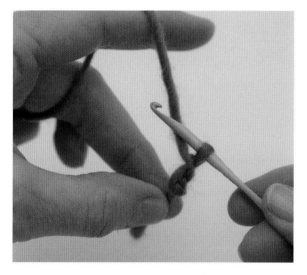

Insert the crochet hook through the loop and pick up the working yarn. Pull the working yarn through the loop to create a new loop.

Keeping the loop on the hook, pick up the working yarn again.

Pull the yarn through to create another loop. Continue this process until the chain is as long as desired. Cut the yarn and pull the yarn tail through the last loop.

Pompoms

Pompoms are just fun. They're great adornments for the tops of hats and edges of scarves. Pompoms can be loose and floppy or very tight and small. They can be made with fine yarns or bulky, or even a mix of different colors or textures. You can be very creative. Before you begin, cut a length of yarn about 12 inches long and set it aside.

Wrap the yarn around your fingers thirty to fifty times. The more times you wrap, the thicker and tighter the pompom will be.

Slip the yarn from your fingers. Wrap and then tie the set-aside length of yarn around the middle as shown. You may want to wrap it around again and re-knot the ends. Later you'll use the tails of the tie to attach the pompom to your project, so don't cut them off.

Cut open the folded ends of the wrapped yarn.

Shake the pompom to fluff the strands. Then trim them to give the pompom a nice round shape. The shorter you cut the strands, the tighter the pompom will look. You can also do the trimming after the pompom is sewn to the knitting.

Fringe

Specific directions for making fringe are given with the projects that include it. But here's the basic method, in case you'd like to add to a design of your own. You may use one to three strands of yarn for each fringe (or more, depending on the weight) and it can be very effective to mix colors or yarn types. One note: Fringe requires a lot of yarn, so if you're adding fringe to a project that does not specify it, purchase extra yarn.

To make fringe, cut a strand of yarn slightly more than twice as long as you want the fringe to be. Fold the strand in half, forming a loop.

Insert a crochet hook through the edge of the project and place the loop in the hook. Pull the loop through the project, then insert the cut ends of the strand through it and pull snug against the edge.

Repeat to add as much fringe as you like. Lay the project flat and use scissors to trim the ends of the fringe so they are even.

Tassels

Tassels can be used as accents at corners of afghans, shawls, or pillows. They are also great to use as hat toppers and at the ends of drawstrings. They are quick and easy to create and can be made in many sizes—your choice, depending on the effect desired. Before you begin, cut a length of yarn about 24 inches long and set it aside to use to tie and wrap the tassel later.

Decide how long the tassels should be, including about 1 inch for the topknot. Cut a piece of cardboard that length. Wrap the yarn around the cardboard twenty to thirty times. The more times you wrap, the thicker the tassel will be.

When you've finished wrapping, cut off the remaining yarn. Fold the set-aside length of yarn in half and lay it on a table. Cut the wrapped yarn at one end of the cardboard. Keeping the other end of the wraps folded, slide the yarn off the cardboard and lay it on the doubled, set-aside strand of yarn. Tie the doubled strand around the wrapped yarn about 1 inch from the folded end (you can use a single strand if you prefer).

This is what the tassel looks like when tied. You can sew the top fold to your project later or slide another strand of yarn through the loop and tie it on.

Wrap the ends of the tied strand around the tassel several times. Then tie off or slide under the wrap to secure.

Hold the tassel by its topknot and, with scissors, trim the loose end to be even. Cut a strand of yarn (or sewing twine, page 81) and slide it through the topknot. Tie the tassel to your project with this yarn.

tip:

If you like, you can fashion a tassel through a buttonhole. To do this, wrap the yarn around the cardboard as usual. When you cut and remove it, insert it through the buttonhole and then fold it double, bringing the cut ends together. Now wrap and tie the topknot close to the edge of your knitting.

The Projects

Ready to put your knitting board to work? Here are more than thirty projects to make for yourself or for gifts. They range from very simple and quick to more complex, and include designs for babies and toddlers, women's fashions, and several home accessories. Each is ranked with a recommended degree of experience needed, but none is very difficult, so we encourage you to try whichever you feel you're ready to do.

Fast & Fun

If you're looking for something quick and easy, or if you are just beginning, here are projects that knit up quickly, no matter what your skills are.

QUICK & EASY COASTERS

These little coasters make a great gift, and they're the perfect exercise for learning the Rib Stitch. Each one takes only a small amount of yarn, so raid your scrap bag. We like to make them in assorted colors and tie sets of four together with a length of crocheted yarn.

SKILL
Very easy

SIZE
About 4 inches square

NEEDED
Knitting board, fine gauge (16+ needles), with ¼ inch between the boards

Knit hook

Crochet hook, size 4/E

YARN
Sport- or worsted-weight yarn, about 20 yards for 1 coaster

STITCH
Rib (page 30)

GAUGE
4 stitches and 4 rows = 1 inch

Coaster

Cast on 16 stitches using the Anchor Yarn method (page 21). Work in Rib Stitch for 16 rows. Remove the coaster from the board using the Soft Crochet (Two-Loop) Bind-Off (page 64). At the cast-on edge, Bind Off to Remove the Anchor Yarn (page 66); pull out the anchor yarn. Pull any yarn tails in between the knit layers.

Finishing

If you wish to tie a set of coasters together as shown in the photo, refer to Drawstrings and Ties (page 83) to make a crochet chain about 4 feet long. Then stack your coasters, wrap the chain around them, and tie a bow. Cute gift!

LOLLY TOTE BAG

Here's a quick and easy project that's great for beginners. The front and back of this bag are knit as one long piece and folded in half for the bottom; the handle is a separate piece sewn on at the end.

SKILL
Very Easy

SIZE
7 inches high by 9 inches wide, with a 10-inch-long handle

NEEDED
Knitting board, small gauge (22+ needles), with ½ inch between the boards

Knit hook

Crochet hook, size 5/H

Large sewing needle

YARN
Premier Yarns *Harmony*, 3½ ounces/100g per ball, each approximately 109 yards/100m (acrylic/wool blend): 1 ball #34-201 Playtime. Or use any bulky-weight yarn you like.

STITCH
Stockinette (page 27)

GAUGE
5 stitches and 6 rows = 2 inches

Bag body

Cast on 22 stitches using the Anchor Yarn method (page 21). Work in Stockinette Stitch for 44 rows. Remove the piece from the board using the Soft Crochet (Two-Loop) Bind-Off (page 64). At the cast-on end, Bind Off to Remove the Anchor Yarn (page 66). Set the piece aside.

Handle

Cast on 22 stitches using the Anchor Yarn method. Work in Stockinette Stitch for 10 rows. Remove the handle from the board using the Soft Crochet (Two-Loop) Bind-Off. At the cast-on end, Bind Off to Remove the Anchor Yarn; pull out the anchor yarn.

Finishing

Fold the bag in half so that the bound-off edges meet; they will form the top edge of the bag. Use 1 strand of yarn to sew each side edge closed using Invisible Stitch (page 79). Fold the handle in half lengthwise and sew the long edges together using small Whipstitches (page 80). Sew the handle so that it has some stretch but maintains its shape. Curve the handle, seam down, and invert it over the bag, placing the ends inside each side seam. Sew each end of the handle to the top edge of the bag using short Topstitches (page 81). Pull any yarn ends in between the knit layers. The tote is ready to use!

LADIES' SNUG SLIPPERS

Comfort and warmth are what slippers are all about. These are so quickly knit in one piece, from the toe to the heel, they make a great stocking stuffer for all the women on your holiday list. You can use either worsted or bulky yarn; the weight difference doesn't affect the size.

SKILL
Easy

SIZE
Small (shoe 5 and 6)

Medium (shoe 7 and 8)

Large/Extralarge (shoe 9, 10, and 11)

Directions for sizes medium and large/extralarge appear in parentheses following size small.

NEEDED
Knitting board, small gauge (22+ needles), with ½ inch between the boards

Knit hook

Crochet hook, Size 5/H

Large sewing needle

YARN
Brown Sheep *Lamb's Pride Worsted,* 4 ounces/113g per skein, each approximately 190 yards/174m (wool/mohair): 2 skeins #M197 Red Hot Passion. Or use any bulky- or worsted-weight yarn you like.

STITCHES
Open Rib (page 32) and Stockinette (page 27)

GAUGE
3 stitches and 3 rows = 1 inch

Slippers

Knit 2 alike. For each, cast on 22 stitches using the Anchor Yarn Method (page 21); use a matching anchor yarn.

Work in Open Rib Stitch for 8 (12,16) rows.

Change to Stockinette Stitch: On the side of the board that has the Open Rib surface, lift 1 loop from each needle that has 2 loops and transfer it to the adjacent empty needle (so that all needles have 1 loop and are directly across from the corresponding needle on the opposite board).

Knit 14 (16,22) rows in Stockinette Stitch. Cut the yarn, leaving a 2-inch-long tail. Remove the slipper from the board using the Soft Crochet (Two-Loop) Bind-Off (page 64).

Finishing

Referring to the photo, fold one slipper in half lengthwise, so the anchor yarn is at one end (the toe) and the bound-off edge is at the other end (the heel). Sew the back-heel seam using a double strand of yarn and Invisible Stitch (page 79); cut and knot the sewing yarn. Sew the top of the slipper from the toe all the way along the Open Braid section and along the Stockinette section for 1 inch. Cut and knot the yarn. Tie the anchor yarn to itself snugly, sliding all the cast-on stitches together, and then cut the yarn, leaving short tails. Pull all the tails in between the knit layers. Sew the other slipper together in the same way.

Drawstrings

Refer to Drawstrings and Ties (page 83), to crochet two 18- to 20-inch-long drawstrings. Weave one around the top of each slipper using the crochet hook as a guide. Tie each in a bow.

ADORABLE BABY BOOTIES

Each bootie is knit in one piece. This is a fun pattern for new knitters and a simple project for learning to shape a knitted piece and maintain the stitch pattern. Besides, babies' feet are so cute!

SKILL
Easy

SIZE
3 to 9 months

NEEDED
Knitting board, small gauge (26+ needles), with ½ inch between the boards

Knit hook

Large sewing needle

Crochet hook, size 3.25/D or 4/G

Satin ribbon (¼ inch wide), 24 inches

YARN
Bernat *Baby Coordinates Chunky,* 3½ ounces/100g per ball, approximately 203 yards/185m (acrylic/rayon/nylon): 1 ball #99435 Cuddly Cameo. Or any chunky-weight yarn you like.

STITCH
Rib Stitch (page 30)

GAUGE
3 stitches and 3½ rows = 1 inch

tip:

If you want the booties to fit very tiny feet, lace some yarn lengthwise through the toe and top and draw up. Then as the baby's feet grow, you can remove this yarn to enlarge the bootie at its full size.

Booties
Knit 2 alike. For each, cast on 24 stitches using the Anchor Yarn method (page 21).

Rows 1–8: Work in Rib Stitch.

Row 9: Bind off 2 stitches at each end (see Bind Off in Pattern, page 65; and Partial Row Bind-Off, page 63). Work the row in Rib Stitch.

Row 10: Work in Rib Stitch.

Row 11: Decrease 1 stitch at each end. Work the row in Rib Stitch, starting on needles #2 and #4.

Row 12: Decrease 1 stitch at each end. Work the row in Rib Stitch, starting on needles #1 and #3.

Rows 13–15: Work straight in Rib Stitch.

Row 16: Increase 1 stitch at each end. Work the row in Rib Stitch starting on needles #2 and #4.

Rows 17–19: Work straight in Rib Stitch.

Remove the bootie from the board using the Soft Crochet (Two-Loop) Bind-Off (page 64); work loosely. At the starting edge, Bind Off to Remove Anchor Yarn (page 66), working loosely again; pull out the anchor yarn.

Finishing
Fold each bootie in half vertically (the cast-on edge is the sole). Using Invisible Stitch (page 79) sew together along the bottom, toe, and front edges. Pull any yarn tails in between the knit layers. Make a pompom for each bootie, wrapping the yarn around your fingers about 35 times (see page 84). Tie the pompoms to the booties, as shown. Cut the ribbon into two 12-inch lengths and thread one through each bootie for a drawstring (use the large sewing needle to guide the ribbon, being careful to pass it between the stitches without piercing the yarn).

RIBBED TURTLENECK SKI VEST

A snappy garment that gives a bit of extra warmth, this vest is fun to make and offers a good way to learn to decrease in a pattern stitch. The front and back are identical. Before beginning, refer to Increasing and Decreasing in Pattern Stitches (page 58), being sure to read the paragraph about Rib Stitch.

SKILL
Intermediate

SIZES
Junior small/medium (medium/large)

Directions for sizes medium/large appear in parentheses following size small/medium.

SKI VEST DIMENSIONS
Measurements are taken with sweater lying flat. All measurements are approximate.

Junior	small/med	med/large
Chest (width at underarm)	17"	19"
Hemline (width at hip)	18"	21"
Length (shoulder to hem)	19"	21"
Shoulders (top width between armhole edges)	14"	15"

NEEDED

Knitting board, small gauge (70+ needles), with ½ inch between the boards

Knit hook

Crochet hook, size 5/F

Large sewing needle

YARN
Lion Brand *Vanna's Choice*, 3½ ounces/100g per ball, approximately 170 yards/156m (acrylic/rayon): 5 (6) balls #108 Dusty Blue for the body; 2 balls #145 Eggplant for the bottom border.

STITCH
Rib Stitch (page 30)

GAUGE
3 stitches and 4 rows = 1 inch

Front and Back

Knit 2 alike. For each, working with eggplant yarn, cast on 58 (68) stitches in Rib Stitch using an Anchor Yarn (page 21).

Work 14 rows in Rib Stitch.

Row 15: Decrease 1 stitch at each end on both boards. Work the row, starting at needle #2 on the top board and weaving down to needle #4 on the bottom board.

Work straight as established for 4 (6) more rows. Cut and knot the yarn. Tie on the blue yarn (see Tying on a New Color, page 48). Work another 25 (29) rows.

Next row: Decrease 1 stitch at each end on both boards. Work the row, starting at needle #1 on the top board and weaving down to needle #3 on the bottom board.

Work straight as established for 12 more rows.

DECREASE FOR ARMHOLES

On each of the next 4 rows, decrease 1 stitch at each end on both boards and then work the row.

Maintain the Rib Stitch pattern as you decrease.

Work straight as established for 22 (26) more rows.

Shape Shoulders and Collar: On each of the next 5 rows, decrease 1 stitch at each end on both boards, then work the row.

Maintain the Rib Stitch pattern as you decrease.

For the collar, continue straight as established for 21 more rows. Remove the knitting from the board using the Soft Crochet (Two-Loop) Bind-Off (page 64). At the cast-on edge, Bind Off to Remove the Anchor Yarn (page 66), being sure to maintain the pattern. Pull out the anchor yarn.

Finishing

Place the front on top of the back, aligning all the edges. Using Invisible Stitch (page 79) and changing colors to match the garment, sew each side seam from bottom to top; at the top, return for a short distance so the knot isn't right at the armhole. Sew each shoulder/collar seam. Pull any yarn tails in between the knit layers.

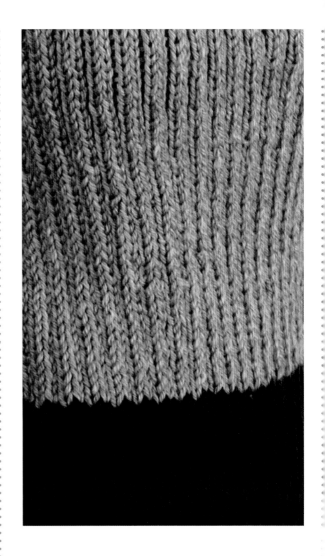

Home
Cozies

The double-faced fabric created on a knitting board is perfect for home accessories. Here are four projects that are fun to make. Each will add a cheerful, cozy accent to your home.

HOMESPUN AFGHAN

Luxurious and cozy, this afghan is sure to be one of your favorites. Knit in one piece, it's easy to do and well worth the time and yarn invested. We used a bouclé yarn that knits up like a bulky weight.

SKILL
Easy

SIZE
Approximately 44 inches wide by 70 inches long without fringe; 96 inches long with fringe

NEEDED
Knitting board, small gauge (84+ needles), with 1 inch between the boards

Knit hook

Crochet hook, size 5mm/H

YARN
Lion Brand *Homespun*, 6 ounces/170g per skein, 185 yards/169m (acrylic/polyester): 10 skeins #790–395 Meadow. Or use any bulky-weight yarn you like.

STITCH
Stockinette (page 27)

GAUGE
2 stitches and 2½ rows = 1 inch

Afghan

Cast on 84 stitches using the Anchor Yarn method (page 21). Work in Stockinette Stitch for a total of 200 rows or until the afghan is the length you desire. Be sure to reserve 2 skeins of yarn for the fringe. Remove the afghan from the board using the Soft Crochet (Two-Loop) Bind-Off (page 64); work very loosely. At the starting end, Bind Off to Remove the Anchor Yarn (page 66), working loosely again; pull out the anchor yarn.

Fringe

Use an entire skein of yarn to prepare the fringe for one end of the afghan. Wrap the yarn around a box or waste can that measures approximately 24 inches around. With scissors, make a straight cut through the wrapped yarn, gathering one end of the strands in your hand as you do so. Wrap some tape around this end or tie it, to keep the pieces tidy. Work with 2 strands at a time to make the fringe as follows: Slip the crochet hook into the first stitch at one end of the afghan. Fold 2 strands of yarn in half over the hook and pull the hook through the stitch (we folded the yarn unevenly, for a more casual look). Remove the hook and pass the strand ends through the folded loop; pull snugly. Repeat to add fringe to each remaining stitch across the end, working about halfway across and then working back from the opposite edge in the same way. Use the remaining skein of yarn to add fringe to the other end of the afghan in the same way, and then repeat on the opposite end. Relax now, wrapped in your cozy afghan!

BOLD STRIPE PILLOW COVER

Slip this over a big soft pillow and toss it onto your sofa or bed, then settle in for a good, comfy read. We chose rich contrasting colors, but this will also look great in a subtle palette of related hues. Or you could visit your leftover-yarn basket and use as many prettily coordinating colors as you find there. Read Horizontal Stripes (page 47) before you begin.

SKILL

Easy

SIZE

Approximately 22 inches square

NEEDED

Knitting board, small gauge (68+ needles), with ½ inch between the boards

Knit hook

Crochet hook, size 5/F

Large sewing needle

22-inch square pillow insert

YARN

Brown Sheep *Lamb's Pride Worsted,* 4 ounces/ 113g per skein, each approximately 190 yards/174m (wool/mohair blend): 1 skein each #M01 Sandy Heather (tan); #M26 Medieval Red (rust); #M81 Red Baron (orange); and #M165 Christmas Green (green). Or use any worsted-weight yarn you like. (To make the cover back a solid color, purchase an additional skein of that color.)

STITCHES

Stockinette (page 27) and Open Rib (page 32)

GAUGE

3 stitches and 4 rows = 1 inch

tip:

It would be fun to add a tassel to each corner when you've finished (see page 86). Make them of mixed colors or a single color.

Pillow Cover

Note: When changing colors, tie on the new color at the beginning of the row and then cut and tie the old color.

Make 2 pieces alike. For each, cast on 68 stitches in tan yarn using the Anchor Yarn method (page 21). Work 10 rows in Stockinette Stitch.

Stripe 2: Change to rust yarn and work 8 rows in Stockinette Stitch.

Stripe 3: Change to orange yarn and work 4 rows in Stockinette Stitch.

Stripe 4: Change to green yarn and work 2 rows in Stockinette Stitch.

Stripe 5: Change to rust and work 8 rows in Open Rib Stitch.

Stripe 6: Change to tan and work 6 rows in Stockinette Stitch.

Stripe 7: Change to orange and work 8 rows in Stockinette Stitch.

Stripe 8: Change to green and work 2 rows in Stockinette Stitch.

Stripe 9: Change to tan and work 8 rows in Stockinette Stitch.

Stripe 10: Change to rust and work 8 rows in Open Rib Stitch.

Stripe 11: Change to orange and work 4 rows in Stockinette Stitch.

Stripe 12: Change to green and work 4 rows in Stockinette Stitch.

Stripe 13: Change to tan and work 10 rows in Stockinette Stitch.

Remove the piece from the board using the Soft Crochet (Two-Loop) Bind-Off (page 64). At the cast-on edge, Bind Off to Remove the Anchor Yarn (page 66). Pull the yarn ends between the knit layers.

Finishing

Arrange the two pieces back-to-back with the Open Rib Stitches facing out and the stripes matching at the edges. Using Invisible Stitch (page 79) and changing colors to match the stripes, sew them together along three edges. Slide the pillow insert between the pieces and then sew the remaining edge closed. Pull any remaining yarn ends in between the knit layers.

SHADES OF GREEN AFGHAN

Cool shades of green make this cozy afghan a perfect accent piece. Two center panels feature alternating stripes of dark and light green—with the pattern stitch alternating, too—and two end panels are all dark, all one stitch. We love it in green for the fall, but, of course, it will be lovely in any color combination you choose.

SKILL
Intermediate

SIZE
Approximately 34 inches wide by 54 inches long

NEEDED
Knitting board, small gauge (68+ needles), with ½ inch between the boards

Knit hook

Crochet hook, size 4/E or 5/H

Large sewing needle

YARN
Brown Sheep *Lamb's Pride Superwash Worsted*, 3½ ounces/100g per skein, 200 yards/183m (washable wool): 5 skeins #SW16 Seafoam (light green); 5 skeins #SW18 Lichen (dark green). Or use any worsted-weight yarn you like.

STITCHES
Stockinette Stitch (page 27) and Crisscross Stitch (page 39)

GAUGE
9 stitches and 12 rows = 3 inches

Center Panels

Knit 2 alike. For each, using dark-green yarn, cast on 68 stitches in Crisscross Stitch (start with Weave Pattern 1, on needles #1 and #4) using an Anchor Yarn (page 21). Work 20 rows in Crisscross Stitch. Cut and knot the yarn.

Tie on light-green yarn (see Tying on a New Color, page 48). Work 30 rows in Stockinette Stitch. Cut and knot the yarn. Tie on dark green. Work 30 rows in Crisscross Stitch. Cut and knot the yarn. Tie on light green. Work 30 rows in Stockinette Stitch. Cut and knot the yarn. Tie on dark green. Work 20 rows in Crisscross Stitch.

Remove the piece from the board using the Soft Crochet (Two-Loop) Bind-Off (page 64); work very loosely. At the starting end, Bind Off to Remove the Anchor Yarn (page 66), working loosely again; pull out the anchor yarn.

End Panels

Knit 2 alike. For each, using dark green, cast on 20 stitches in Crisscross Stitch using an anchor yarn (as for the center panels). Work 130 rows in Crisscross Stitch (or work until the piece is the same length as the center panels). Remove the piece from the board using the Soft Crochet (Two-Loop) Bind-Off; work very loosely. At the cast-on end, Bind Off to Remove the Anchor Yarn, working loosely again; pull out the anchor yarn.

Finishing

Using Invisible Stitch (page 79) and changing colors to match the stripes, sew the center panels together along one long edge. Then, using dark green, sew an end panel to each remaining long edge of the center. Pull any yarn tails in between the knit layers. Your warm blanket is done and will look pretty draped over a sofa—or over you!

SUMMER STRIPES RUG

Get started knitting beautiful double-knit rugs for your home with this classic design, which is knit from side to side with simple horizontal stripes. The stripes are fun and, in bright colors like these, so cheery. Cast on fewer stitches if you'd like a shorter rug, and if you'd like one that's wider, just keep making stripes. Read Horizontal Stripes (page 47) before you begin.

tip:

The rug is 67 rows wide—you can vary the stripe widths any way you like. Knit more or wider stripes to make a wider rug, or fewer to make a narrower one.

SKILL
Easy

SIZE
20 inches wide by 40 inches long, including fringe

NEEDED
Knitting board, small gauge (84+ needles), with ½ inch between the boards

Knit hook

Crochet hook, size 6/G

YARN
Lion Brand *Wool-Ease Thick & Quick,* 6 ounces/170g per ball, approximately 106 yards/97m (acrylic/wool): 3 balls #640–138 Cranberry (red); 3 balls #640–132 Lemongrass (green). Or use any superbulky-weight yarn you like.

STITCH
Stockinette (page 27)

GAUGE
2 inches and 3 rows = 1 inch

Rug

Note: Work the rug entirely in Stockinette Stitch. When changing colors, tie on the new color at the beginning of the row and then cut and tie the old one.

With red yarn, cast on 84 stitches in Stockinette Stitch using an Anchor Yarn (page 21). *Note: When casting on with a large number of stitches, it helps to place two anchor yarns instead of one. Place the first across the first half of the stitches and the second across the remaining stitches. This will make it easier to move the first few rows of knitting down between the boards.*

Work 6 rows.

Change to green yarn and work 3 rows.
Change to red and work 5 rows.
Change to green and work 4 rows. Change to red and work 7 rows.
Repeat from * to * once.
Change to green and work 6 rows.
Change to red and work 6 rows.
Repeat from * to * once.
Change to green and work 3 rows.
Change to red and work 5 rows.

Remove the rug from the board using the Soft Crochet (Two-Loop) Bind-Off (page 64). At the cast-on edge, Bind Off to Remove the Anchor Yarn(s) (page 66); pull out the anchor yarn. Pull the yarn tails in between the knit layers.

Fringe

Cut 134 strands of green yarn, each 7 inches long. Add one strand to each stitch at each end of the rug as follows: Slip the crochet hook into the first stitch at one end of the rug. Fold a strand of yarn in half over the hook and pull the hook through the stitch. Remove the hook and pass the strand ends through the folded loop; pull snug. Repeat on each remaining stitch across the end and then on the opposite end. When finished, lay the rug flat and use scissors to trim the fringe ends to be even. Your rug is ready to go.

Hats,
Scarves,
and
Mittens

Warm the heads, necks, and fingers of everyone you love with the winter accessories in this chapter. Some are supereasy, others take some skill. So take your pick—you're sure to find something to suit everyone on your gift list and yourself as well.

SIERRA HAT & SCARF

This fun hat-and-scarf set is knit in Rib Stitch with easy horizontal stripes. These are great pieces for advanced beginners who want to try working with multiple colors. And when finished, they're a great design for the guys—make them in team colors to promote the sporting spirit. Read Horizontal Stripes (page 47) before beginning.

SKILL
Easy

SIZE
The scarf is approximately 5 inches wide by 56 inches long. The hat is about 26 inches in circumference, to fit most adults.

NEEDED
Knitting board, small gauge (68+ needles), with ½ inch between the boards

Knit hook

Crochet hook, size 5/F or 6/G

Large sewing needle

YARN
Brown Sheep *Lamb's Pride Bulky*, 4 ounces/113g per skein, each approximately 125 yards/114m (wool/mohair): 3 skeins #M03 Grey Heather (gray, the main color); 1 skein #M29 Jack's Plum (purple); 1 skein #M220 Ocean Waves (blue). Or use any bulky-weight yarn you like.

STITCH
Rib Stitch (page 30)

GAUGE
9 stitches and 10 rows = 3 inches

Scarf

Cast on 18 stitches with gray yarn in Rib Stitch using the Anchor Yarn method (page 21). Work 3 rows in Rib Stitch. At the beginning of the next row, tie on purple yarn between the second and third needles (see Horizontal Stripes, page 47). Do not cut the gray yarn.

Work 3 rows with purple. Then knot and cut the purple, leaving a 3-inch-long tail.

Pick up the gray and work 1 row. Then cut the gray, leaving a 3-inch-long tail.

Tie on blue yarn and work 6 rows. Then cut the blue.

Tie on the purple; work 4 rows. Do not cut the yarn.

Tie on the gray; work 1 row. Do not cut the yarn.

Pick up the purple; work 2 rows. Cut the purple.

Pick up the gray; work 4 rows. Cut the gray.

Tie on the blue; work 3 rows. Cut the blue.

Tie on the purple; work 3 rows. Cut the purple.

Tie on the gray. Work for 36 inches. Cut the gray; tie on the purple.

Work the stripe pattern in reverse sequence. End with 4 rows of gray instead of 3 rows; then cut the gray leaving a 3-inch-long tail. Remove the scarf from the board using the Soft Crochet (Two-Loop) method (page 64). At the starting end, Bind Off to Remove the Anchor Yarn (page 66); pull out the anchor yarn. Pull any yarn tails in between the knit layers.

Hat

The hat is knit from the top of the crown to the edge of the cuff in Rib Stitch. When you cast on, use a matching double strand of yarn for the anchor yarn, as it will remain in the finished hat.

Cast on 68 stitches in gray yarn in Rib Stitch using an Anchor Yarn (page 21).

Work 12 rows in Rib Stitch; then cut and knot the gray.

Tie on blue yarn; work 4 rows. Cut and knot the blue.

Tie on the gray; work 2 rows. Cut the gray.

Tie on the purple; work 6 rows. Cut and knot the purple.

Tie on the gray; work 18 rows—the last 6 rows will turn up to form the cuff. Remove the hat from the board using the Soft Crochet (Two-Loop) method.

Finishing

Fold the hat so the anchor yarn is at one end and the bound-off (brim) edge is at the other, and pin the short side edges together.

Working from the cuff to the top, sew the side seam with Invisible Stitch (page 79).

Cut and knot the sewing yarn at the top.

Tie the anchor yarn to itself snugly, sliding all the cast-on stitches together, and then cut the yarn, leaving short tails.

Pull the tails in between the knit layers. Fold up the brim. Add a pompom (page 84). Very cool!

SOFT ALPACA SCARF

So easy to knit up, this scarf is a perfect starting point for new knitting-board knitters. It can be made in brighter colors, changing the look entirely, or accented with a different color yarn for the fringe. Just remember—to keep the side edges even, make sure to work the knitting from both outside edges into the middle, instead of back and forth. This creates an even, straight edge on both sides of the scarf from top to bottom.

SKILL
Very Easy

SIZE
Approximately 7 inches wide by 34 inches long, including fringe

NEEDED
Knitting board, small gauge (22+ needles), with ½ inch between the boards

Knit hook

Crochet hook, size 4/E

YARN
Plymouth *Baby Alpaca DK*, 1¾ ounces/50g per ball, 125 yds/114m (baby alpaca) 3 balls #1477 green. Or use any DK-weight yarn you like.

STITCH
Stockinette (page 27)

GAUGE
6 stitches and 7 rows = 2 inches

Scarf

Cast on 22 stitches in Stockinette Stitch using an Anchor Yarn (page 21). Work in Stockinette Stitch for 90 rows, until the scarf is 26 inches long. Remove the scarf from the board using the Soft Crochet (Two-Loop) Bind-Off (page 64). At the starting end, Bind Off to Remove the Anchor Yarn (page 66); pull out the anchor yarn.

FRINGE

Cut 88 strands of yarn, each 9 inches long. Using 2 strands together, make the fringe as follows: Slip the crochet hook into the first stitch at one end of the scarf. Fold 2 strands of yarn in half over the hook and pull the hook through the stitch. Remove the hook and pass the strand ends through the folded loop; pull snug. Repeat on each remaining stitch across the end and then on the opposite end. When finished, lay the scarf flat and use scissors to trim the fringe ends to be even. Your scarf is ready to wear.

tip:

Depending on the yarn you're using, you might like the fringe to be thicker. If so, cut 132 strands and use 3 together for each piece of fringe.

tip:

Depending on the yarn you're using, you might like the fringe to be thicker. If so, cut 120 strands and use 2 together for each piece of fringe.

RIBBED HAT
& SCARF

This is a wonderful set that becomes so special when made in a beautiful yarn, and the long fringe gives it a classy finish. We show it in a lovely soft bouclé; this pattern also works well in fine to medium-weight chenille or velour, or any classic worsted-weight yarn. If you want to add a pompom to the hat, be sure to buy more yarn than indicated.

SKILL
Easy

SIZE
The scarf is approximately 9 inches wide by 82 inches long, including 6-inch-long fringe at both ends. The hat is 26 inches in circumference, to fit most adults.

NEEDED
Knitting board, small gauge (60+ needles), with ½ inch between the boards

Knit hook

Crochet hook, size 5/H

Large sewing needle

YARN
Bernat *Soft Bouclé*, 5 ounces/140g per ball, approximately 255 yards/233m (acrylic/polyester): 2 balls #26948 Slate Shades (300 yards for the scarf, 150 yards for the hat). Or use any bulky-weight yarn you like.

STITCHES
Rib (page 30) and Open Rib (page 32)

GAUGE
3 stitches and 3 rows = 1 inch

Scarf

Cast on 30 stitches in Rib Stitch using an Anchor Yarn (page 21). Work in Rib Stitch for 228 rows or until the scarf is as long as desired. Remove the scarf from the board using the Soft Crochet (Two-Loop) Bind-Off (page 64). At the cast-on end, Bind Off to Remove the Anchor Yarn (page 66). Pull out the anchor yarn. Pull any yarn tails in between the knit layers.

FRINGE

Cut 60 strands of yarn, each 14 inches long. Add 1 strand to each stitch at each end of the scarf as follows: Slip the crochet hook into the first stitch at one end of the scarf. Fold a strand of yarn in half over the hook and pull the hook through the stitch. Remove the hook and pass the strand ends through the folded loop; pull snug. Repeat on each remaining stitch across the end and then on the opposite end. When finished, lay the scarf flat and use scissors to trim the fringe ends to be even. Your scarf is ready to wear!

Hat

The hat is knit from the top of the crown to the brim in Rib Stitch, and the brim is worked in Open Rib Stitch. When you cast on, use a matching double strand of yarn for the anchor yarn, as it will remain in the finished hat.

Cast on 60 stitches in Rib Stitch using an Anchor Yarn. Work in Rib Stitch for 30 rows.

CUFF

Change to Open Rib Stitch and work 12 more rows. Remove the hat from the board using the Soft Crochet (Two-Loop) Bind-Off.

Finishing

Fold the hat so that the anchor yarn is at one end and the Open Rib Stitch face of the cuff is on the inside, and pin the short side edges together. Working from the cuff to the top, sew the side seam with Invisible Stitch (page 79). Cut and knot the sewing yarn at the top. Tie the anchor yarn to itself snugly, sliding all the cast-on stitches together, and then cut the yarn, leaving short tails. Pull the tails in between the knit layers. Fold up the cuff to reveal the Open Rib Stitch. If you wish, add a pompom (page 84). Very chic!

LOOPY RIB SCARF

This soft scarf gets its chunky look from the Loopy Rib Stitch, which creates a gentle scallop along the cast-on edge. To create that scallop on both ends of the scarf, knit two pieces—each half the total length—and then sew their bound-off edges together. Whether made in one or two pieces, this knits up quickly and is fun for anyone with advanced-beginner skills.

SKILL
Intermediate

SIZE
6 inches wide by 36 inches long

NEEDED
Knitting board, small gauge (24+ needles), with ½ inch between the boards

Knit hook

Crochet hook, size 6/G

Large sewing needle (for two-piece version)

YARN
Lion Brand *Wool-Ease Thick & Quick*, 6 ounces/170g per ball, 106 yards/97m (acrylic/wool): 2 balls #640–114 Denim. Or use any superbulky-weight yarn you like.

STITCH
Loopy Rib (page 35)

GAUGE
2 stitches and 2 rows = 1 inch

One-Piece Scarf

Note: The bound-off edge of the one-piece scarf is not quite as scalloped as the cast-on edge.

Cast on 12 stitches in Loopy Rib Stitch using an Anchor Yarn (page 21). Work in Loopy Rib Stitch for 74 rows. Bind Off in Pattern (page 35) using Rib Stitch. To finish the cast-on edge, simply pull out the anchor yarn. Pull any yarn tails in between the knit layers. That's it!

Two-Piece Scarf

Make 2 pieces alike. For each, cast on 12 stitches in Loopy Rib Stitch using an Anchor Yarn. Work in Loopy Rib Stitch for 36 rows. Bind Off in Pattern using Rib Stitch. Sew the pieces together along the bound-off edges with Invisible Stitch (page 79), making sure to match the ribs. To finish the cast-on edges, simply pull out each anchor yarn. Pull any yarn tails in between the knit layers. That's it!

tip:

When working this stitch, focus on the previous row of knitting to guide your weaving—each row should mirror the previous row.

Beautiful merino wool yarn makes this classic scarf-and-hat duo an eye-catcher. You could use a different type of bulky-weight yarn, but merino is so soft you're sure to love wearing it. The scarf is worked in alternating bands of Stockinette and Rib stitches. And the hat is a strip of Rib Stitch only, turned sideways so the ribs are horizontal when worn, which means you can customize the size by knitting a strip that is just long enough to wrap around the head of the wearer.

MERINO HAT & SCARF

SKILL
Intermediate

SIZE
The scarf is approximately 9 inches wide by 74 inches long, including 7-inch fringe at each end. The hat is knit to the desired size.

NEEDED
Knitting board, small gauge (40+ needles), with ½ inch between the boards

Knit hook

Crochet hook, size 5/H

Large sewing needle

YARN
Brown Sheep *Lamb's Pride Bulky*, 4 ounces/113g per skein, each approximately 125 yards/114m (wool/mohair blend): 6 skeins #M10 Creme for both projects or 3 skeins for each one. Or use any bulky-weight yarn you like.

STITCHES
Stockinette (page 27) and Rib (page 30)

GAUGE
6 stitches and 7 rows = 2 inches

Scarf
Cast on 30 stitches using the Anchor Yarn method (page 21). Work in Rib Stitch for 6 rows. Change to Stockinette Stitch and work 6 rows.

Continue in this way to work alternating 6-row bands of each stitch until you have completed 15 sections of Stockinette Stitch and 16 sections of Rib Stitch—the scarf will be approximately 60 inches long. Remove the scarf from the board using the Soft Crochet (Two-Loop) Bind-Off (page 64). At the cast-on end, Bind Off to Remove the Anchor Yarn (page 66). Pull out the anchor yarn. Pull any yarn tails in between the knit layers.

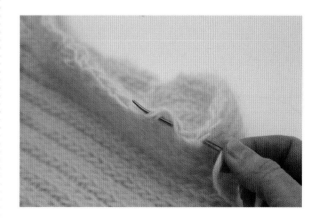

FRINGE

Cut 60 strands of yarn, each 15 inches long. Add one strand to each stitch at each end of the scarf as follows: Slip the crochet hook into the first stitch at one end of the scarf. Fold a strand of yarn in half over the hook and pull the hook through the stitch. Remove the hook and pass the strand ends through the folded loop; pull snug.

Repeat on each remaining stitch across the end and then on the opposite end. When finished, lay the scarf flat and use scissors to trim the fringe ends to be even. Chic and warm!

Hat

Before beginning, measure around the wearer's head at the nape of neck and over the ears. The strip you knit for the hat should be a little less than this measurement in length. The hat is 12 inches high (shown with 2 inches turned up for a cuff). If you'd like a taller hat, cast on an additional 3 stitches for every inch desired; for a shorter hat, subtract 3 stitches for every inch you wish to omit.

Cast on 36 stitches in Rib Stitch using an Anchor Yarn. Work in Rib Stitch until the piece is long enough to wrap snugly around the head (multiply the desired length by 3½—the row gauge—to determine the number of rows). To remove the hat from the board, Bind Off in Pattern (page 35). At the cast-on end, Bind Off to Remove the Anchor Yarn (page 66), making sure to maintain the pattern. (Binding Off in Pattern ensures that the ribs will match nicely when you sew the ends of the strip together.)

Finishing

Fold the hat in half so the cast-on and bound-off edges meet; sew them together with Invisible Stitch (page 79). To form the top of the hat, first cut a 40-inch-long strand of yarn; double it and tie it to one end of the seam. Thread the ends through the needle and weave the needle in and out of the stitches along the top edge of the hat.

Gently slide the stitches together along the yarn to close the top; tie the yarn and cut off the excess. If adding a pompom, leave long tails for tying it on; otherwise, leave short tails and pull them in between the knit layers. Add a pompom (page 84) to the top if you like, wrapping the yarn loosely about 40 times.

CUFF

If you wish, fold up the open end of the hat to form a cuff. To secure it, tack it to the hat in a few places. Charming!

tip:

If you'd like a rolled cuff instead
of a flat one, simply roll the edge
over a few times and sew the roll
loosely to the hat, passing the
sewing yarn invisibly along
the inside of the roll.

EARFLAP HAT & BIG DOTS SCARF

This hat and scarf set will keep your ears and neck cozy warm. Bold stripes look lively and complement the bold circles on the Big Dot Scarf perfectly. The hat knits up in a jiffy: It's worked in one piece from the top down and seamed in the back. Before beginning, read Horizontal Stripes (page 47) and Partial Row Bind-Off (page 63). The two-color design is worked from an easy-to-follow graph that depicts the full width of the scarf, making this a perfect project for learning how add a colorful motif to a plain background. Because the chart shows all the stitches in each row of the motif, it's easy to see when to change the colors. Read the chapter Creating Patterns with Color (page 46) before you begin, being sure to read the sidebar Charted Designs (page 52).

SKILL
Intermediate

SIZE
Hat: approximately 22½ inches in circumference, to fit most adults

Scarf: approximately 6 inches wide by 54 inches long

NEEDED
Hat: Knitting board, small gauge (56+ needles), with ½ inch between the boards

Scarf: Knitting board, small gauge (16+ needles), with ½ inch between the boards

Knit hook

Crochet hook, size 5/F or 6/G (for Hat)

YARN
Hat: Brown Sheep *Lamb's Pride Bulky*, 4 ounces/ 113g per skein, each approximately 125 yards/114m (wool/mohair blend): 1 skein #M124 Persian Peacock (blue); 1 skein #191 Kiwi (green). Or use any bulky-weight yarn you like.

Scarf: Brown Sheep *Lamb's Pride Bulky*, 4 ounces/ 113g per skein, each approximately 125 yards/114m (wool/mohair blend): 1 skein #M124 Persian Peacock (blue); 1 skein #191 Kiwi (green). Or use any bulky-weight yarn you like.

STITCH
Stockinette (page 27)

GAUGE
5 stitches and 6 rows = 2 inches

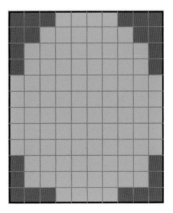

BIG DOT CHART

Hat

Note: The hat is worked entirely in Stockinette Stitch. When changing colors, tie on the new color at the beginning of the row and then cut and tie the old one.

Working with blue yarn, cast on 56 stitches using the Anchor Yarn method (page 21); use a double strand of blue for the anchor yarn. Work 7 rows in blue.

Work 5 rows in green yarn.

Work 5 rows in blue.

Work 5 rows in green.

Work 4 rows in blue.

DIND OFF FOR FOREHEAD EDGE

Bind off the 14 center stitches to create the forehead edge. To do this, count 21 needles from the right end of the board. Then, starting on needle #22, working from right to left with the Soft Crochet (Two-Loop) Bind-Off (page 64), remove the next 14 stitches from the board. Place the loop remaining on your crochet hook on the next needle on one board (needle #21, counting from the left end of the board). From this point the 21 stitches remaining at each end of the board will be worked separately.

FIRST EARFLAP AND BACK NECKLINE

Work the first earflap on the 21 stitches at the left end of the board. Work 1 row on these stitches; when ready to hook over the needle with the extra loop (adjacent to the forehead), lift the 2 bottom loops over the needle.

On the next row, decrease 1 stitch at the right end of the earflap on both boards; work the row. Work 1 more row in blue.

Change to green yarn. On each of the next 4 rows, decrease 1 stitch at the right end of the earflap on both boards; work the row.

On the next row, begin the back neckline: Lay the working yarn between the boards, across the earflap stitches. Then, starting at the left end, bind off the first 8 stitches; place the loop remaining on your crochet hook on needle #9. Work the row. When you hook over the needle with the extra loop, lift the two bottom loops.

On each of the next 2 rows, decrease 1 stitch at each end of the earflap on both boards.

Change to the blue. At each of the next 3 rows, decrease 1 stitch at each end of the earflap on both boards. Remove the flap from the board using the Soft Crochet (Two-Loop) Bind-Off.

SECOND EARFLAP

To work the earflap at the right end of the board, first tie on the blue yarn at the first bound-off stitch of the forehead area. Work the second earflap as you did the first one, but reverse the shaping.

Finishing

Fold the hat so the back edges meet and the stripes match; sew together using matching yarn and the Invisible Stitch (page 79). Cut and knot the sewing yarn. Tie the anchor yarn to itself snugly, sliding all the cast-on stitches together, and then cut the yarn, leaving short tails. Add a pompom to the top if you wish (page 84). Pull the tails in between the knit layers.

Ties

To make a braided tie as shown on the sample, cut three 3-foot-long strands of blue yarn.

Hold them together and, with the crochet hook, pull the ends between the stitches at the bottom of the earflap; tie in a knot inside the flap.

Then braid the strands and tie a knot at the other end.

Repeat for the second tie.

Or, to make a crocheted chain tie for each earflap, cut a 6-foot length of yarn, double it, and use a crochet hook to pull the fold through the end of the earflap. Remove the hook and then pass the ends of the yarn through the folded loop; pull snug. Crochet this double strand to make the tie (see Drawstrings and Ties, page 83). If you like, attach a small pom-pom to the end of each tie. No more chilly ears when the wind blows cold!

Scarf

Working with the blue yarn, cast on 16 stitches using the Anchor Yarn method (page 21). Work in Stockinette Stitch for 5 rows.

Row 6: Tie on the green yarn at needle #6, counting from the left end of the board. Work Row 1 of the Big Dot chart on page 133, working the contrasting stitches on needles #7 through #10. Work the stitches remaining at each edge with blue.

*Rows 7 through 17: In the same way, one row at a time, follow the chart to work the green dot on the center stitches and then work the stitches remaining on each edge in blue. Do not cut the green accent yarn; lay it aside.

Next 3 rows: Work with blue only.

Next row: Pick up the green and work the first row of the chart on the center stitches and the remaining stitches in blue as before.*

Repeat from * to * twice, then repeat Rows 7 through 17 once—for a total of 4 dots.

Work 60 rows in blue for the middle of the scarf.

Next row: Repeat Row 6 to work the first row of a dot.

Repeat from * to * 3 times, then repeat Rows 7 through 17 once—for a total of 4 dots. Then complete the knitting with 5 rows of blue.

Remove the scarf from the board using the Soft Crochet (Two-Loop) Bind-Off. At the cast-on end, Bind Off to Remove the Anchor Yarn (page 66); pull out the anchor yarn. Pull any yarn tails in between the knit layers. Your scarf is ready to wear!

LITTLE KITTENS MITTENS

designed by Faith Smidt

You will find these mittens quick to knit up and wonderfully warm for little hands. They were designed by our friend Faith Smidt and have been "kid-tested" by her seven children, who love them! They come in four sizes, have an extra-long cuff to keep out the snow and cold, and are easily adjusted for a perfect fit. This is a great pattern with which to learn basic shaping. Before beginning, read the chapter Increasing and Decreasing (page 58), being sure to read the section Increasing Inside (page 55).

SKILL
Intermediate

SIZES
Child's Extra-small (Small, Medium, and Large)

Directions for sizes small, medium, and large appear in parentheses following size extra-small.

LITTLE KITTENS MITTENS DIMENSIONS
(Measurements are taken with mittens lying flat. All measurements are approximate.)

Extra-small (2–4 years)
Length (fingertip to edge of cuff) 6½"; Width (across mitten right below the thumb) 3"

Small (5–7 years)
Length 7½"; Width 3¼"

Medium (8–10 years)
Length 8¼"; Width 3⅝"

Large (women's small)
Length 9"; Width 4"

NEEDED
Knitting board, small gauge (26+ needles), with ½ inch between the boards

Knit hook

Crochet hook, size 5/F or 6/G

Large sewing needle

YARN
Patons *Shetland Chunky Tweeds*, 3 ounces/85g per ball, approximately 108 yards/99m (acrylic/wool): 1 (2,2,2) balls #67128 Sea Ice Tweeds. Or use any chunky-weight yarn you like.

STITCHES
Stockinette (page 27) and Rib (page 30)

GAUGE
5 stitches and 7 rows = 2 inches

Mittens

Make 2 alike.

For each, using the needles in the center of your knitting board, cast on 11 (12,13,13) stitches using the Design 8 method (page 23).

Work 6 (7,8,8) rows in Rib Stitch. Work 1 row (all sizes) in Stockinette Stitch.

SHAPE HAND

Work the rest of the mitten in Stockinette Stitch.

Next row: Increase on both boards as follows—size extra-small: 1 stitch in center of work. Sizes small and medium—no increase. Size large—3 stitches evenly spaced across the knitting. Work the row.

Next row: Size medium only—increase 1 stitch in center of work on both boards. All sizes—work the row.

Next 2 rows: Work even as established.

Next row: All sizes increase 1 stitch at each end on both boards—14 (14,16,18) stitches on the board. Work the row.

Now work 1 (2,2,2) more rows.

Next row: Increase 5 (6,6,7) stitches evenly spaced across the row—19 (20,22,25) stitches on the board. Work the row.

Now work even for 2 more rows.

REMOVE STITCHES FOR THUMB

On each board, transfer the center 5 (6,6,7) stitches to a piece of scrap yarn (pull the yarn through the stitches with a crochet hook and then lift them off the needles). Tie the ends of each piece of scrap yarn in a knot. Gently push the removed stitches down between the boards, so that each set hangs below the boards. Shift the stitches remaining on the board over to fill in the empty needles. To reinforce the thumb base, on each board lift the 2 center stitches from their needles (1 from each side of the removed stitches) and transpose them (see Reinforcing Weak Spots, page 30).

SHAPE FINGER AREA

Work even for 5 (6,8,10) more rows.

On each of the next 2 rows, decrease 1 stitch at each end and 2 stitches in the center of the board (all sizes), shift the stitches over to fill the empty needles, and then work the row—6 (6,8,10) stitches remain on the board.

REMOVE THE MITTEN FROM THE BOARD

Cut the working yarn, leaving a 12- to 14-inch-long tail. Thread the tail onto a sewing needle and, starting with the stitch opposite the working yarn and working back and forth across the board, slip each stitch off its needle and onto the sewing needle and yarn tail. Pull the yarn all the way through the stitches and set the mitten aside; later you'll use the yarn tail to sew the side seam.

COMPLETE THE THUMB

Fold the mitten in half lengthwise, right sides together. Line up both sets of thumb stitches (the ones on the scrap yarn) and push them up through the boards from underneath. Carefully place the loops back on the needles, making sure that they are directly across from each other. Some of the last stitches will be a bit tight: Just stretch them gently but firmly—they will go back on. When the stitches are all back on the boards, gently pull out the scrap yarn. Tie on the yarn at needle #2 (see Tying on a New Color, page 48, but use the same yarn).

Work even for 2 (4,5,6) rows.

Next row: Decrease 1 stitch at each end on both boards; work the row.

Cut the working yarn, leaving a 10- to 12-inch-long tail. Thread the tail into the sewing needle and remove the stitches from the board (as you did at the fingertip area).

Finishing

At the top of the thumb, pass the needle with the yarn tail through the stitches in sequence again and pull the yarn snug. Fold the thumb in half lengthwise and sew closed with Invisible Stitch (page 79). In the same way, close the top of the fingertip area and sew the side of the mitten closed. Toasty!

CABLED HAT, SCARF, & MITTENS

Here's a set of beautiful accessories that give a great winter look. Bulky wool makes them very warm and cozy. Lots of cables make this project suitable for anyone ready to try something complex but not difficult on the knitting board. For the scarf you may twist the cables on both the front and back boards if you like, but for the hat and mittens twist them on one board only. Before you begin, read about Cables, beginning on page 41.

SKILL
Intermediate

SIZES
Scarf: approximately 10 inches wide x 68 inches long

Hat: approximately 22 inches in circumference, to fit most adults

Mittens: small/medium and large (see measurements below)

Directions for size large appear in parentheses following size small/medium.

CABLED MITTENS DIMENSIONS
Measurements are taken with mittens lying flat. All measurements are approximate.

Size	Small/med	Large
Length (fingertip to edge of cuff)	11"	12"
Width (across mitten right above the thumb)	3½"	4½"

NEEDED
Knitting board, small gauge (58+ needles), with ½ inch between the boards

Knitting hook

Crochet hook, size 6/G

Large sewing needle

2 stitch holders for cable stitches

YARN
Brown Sheep *Lamb's Pride Bulky*, 4 ounces/113g per skein, each approximately 125 yards/114m (wool/mohair blend): 8 skeins #M10 Creme for the whole set or 5 skeins for the hat or scarf only. Or use any bulky-weight yarn you like.

STITCHES
Stockinette (page 27), Ribbed Cables (page 43), and Open Rib (page 32)

GAUGE
3 stitches and 3 rows = 1 inch overall

WEAVE PATTERNS

The weave patterns set the background of alternating Stockinette and Rib Stitch sections for the scarf and hat. Following is the sequence for setting them up when the project directions indicate it's time to do so. Weave in the sequence given; when you return on each row to make the full circular, if you concentrate on covering the empty needles you won't get mixed up or miss a needle. Once set, continue to work each subsequent row in the Weave Pattern and, at the same time, follow the Cable Pattern described below to twist the cables in the Rib Stitch sections.

Scarf Weave Pattern

4 Stockinette Stitches, 8 Rib Stitches, 6 Stockinette Stitches, 8 Rib Stitches, 4 Stockinette Stitches

Hat Weave Pattern

2 Stockinette Stitches, *8 Rib Stitches, 4 Stockinette Stitches*, repeat from * to * 3 more times, then weave 8 Rib Stitches followed by 2 Stockinette Stitches.

Cable Pattern

The cable sections are worked on 4 Ribs (8 stitches) each, with 4 rows of the Weave Pattern following each Cable Twist row. After you set the Weave Pattern for your project, mark the needles holding each ribbed section by placing a piece of tape in front of them on your knitting board. Work each cable section as follows; count the Ribs from left to right within each section and transpose the stitches before you weave the row.

Twist 1: Transpose Rib 1 with Rib 2 and Rib 3 with Rib 4, placing Ribs 1 and 3 in front.

Twist 2: Transpose Rib 2 with Rib 3, placing Rib 2 in back.

Cabled Scarf

Cast on 30 stitches using the Anchor Yarn method (page 21). Work 1 row in Stockinette Stitch.

Row 2: Set the Scarf Weave Pattern as indicated above, hook over.

Rows 3 and 4: Work 2 rows in the Scarf Weave Pattern.

Row 5—first cable row: Work Cable Twist 1 in each Rib Stitch section and then work the Weave Pattern.

Rows 6 and 7: Repeat rows 3 and 4.

Row 8—second cable row: Work Cable Twist 2 in each Rib Stitch section and then work the Weave Pattern.

Repeat Rows 3 through 8 thirty-two times or until your scarf is nearly the desired length. Then repeat Rows 3 and 4 once more. Working loosely, remove the scarf from the board using the Soft Crochet (Two-Loop) Bind-Off (page 64). At the cast-on edge, Bind Off to Remove the Anchor Yarn (page 66); work loosely and maintain the pattern (see Bind Off in Pattern, page 65). Pull out the anchor yarn. Wrap the scarf around your neck to keep the chill away!

Cabled Hat

The hat is worked from the top to the cuff.

Cast on 60 stitches using the Anchor Yarn method, use a matching anchor yarn.

Row 1: Set the Hat Weave Pattern as indicated; hook over.

Rows 2 and 3: Work 2 rows in the Hat Weave Pattern.

Row 4—first cable row: Work Cable Twist 1 in each Rib Stitch section and then work the Weave Pattern.

Rows 5 and 6: Repeat rows 2 and 3.

Row 7—second cable row: Work Cable Twist 2 in each Rib Stitch section and then work the Weave Pattern.

Repeat rows 2 through 7 three times more.

CUFF

On the side of the board opposite the cables, shift the stitches to set up for Open Rib Stitch. Work 10 rows in Open Rib Stitch. Working loosely, remove the hat from the board using the Soft Crochet (Two-Loop) Bind-Off.

FINISHING

Fold the hat in half so the side edges meet; sew them together using Invisible Stitch (page 79). The cuff will turn up to the outside, so make sure the knots of the sewing yarn will not be visible. Cut and knot the sewing yarn. Tie the anchor yarn to itself snugly, sliding all the cast-on stitches together, and then cut the yarn, leaving short tails. Add a pompom to the top (see page 84). Pull the tails in between the knit layers. Turn up the cuff and the hat is ready to wear!

Mittens

Directions for size large appear in parentheses following size small/medium.

Make 2 alike. For each, using the needles in the center of your knitting board, cast on 22 (24) stitches with Design 8 method (page 23).

Work 12 rows in Rib Stitch.

Work 2 rows in Stockinette Stitch.

SHAPE HAND

Work the rest of the mitten in Stockinette Stitch. Before beginning, read the chapter Increasing and Decreasing (page 54), being sure to read the section Increasing Inside (page 56).

Next row: Increase 1 stitch at each end on both boards; work the row.

Work even as established for 3 (4) more rows.

Next row: Increase 6 stitches evenly spaced across the board; work the row—30 (32) stitches are now on the board.

Work even for 2 (4) more rows.

Next row: Increase 1 stitch at each end on both boards (page 55); work the row.

Work 1 more row.

REMOVE STITCHES FOR THUMB

On each board, transfer the center 8 stitches to a piece of scrap yarn (pull the yarn through the stitches with a crochet hook and then lift them off the needles). Tie the ends of each piece of scrap yarn in a knot. Gently push the removed stitches down between the boards, so that each set hangs below the boards. Shift the stitches remaining on the board over to fill in the empty needles. To reinforce the thumb base, on each board lift the 4 center stitches from their needles (one from each side of the removed stitches) and transpose them (see Reinforcing Weak Spots, page 38).

COMPLETE THE FINGER AREA

Work even for 16 rows. Cut the working yarn, leaving a 12- to 14-inch-long tail. Lay the tail across the stitches between the boards (like an anchor yarn). Remove the mitten from the board using the Soft Crochet (Two-Loop) Bind-Off (page 64). Leave the yarn tail so you can sew the side seam with it later.

COMPLETE THE THUMB

Fold the mitten in half lengthwise, right sides together. Line up both sets of thumb stitches (the ones on the scrap yarn) and push them up through the boards from underneath. Carefully place the loops back on the needles, making sure that they are directly across from each other. Some of the last stitches will be a bit tight: Just stretch them gently but firmly—they will go back on. When the stitches are all back on the boards, gently pull out the scrap yarn. Tie on the yarn at needle #2 (see Tying on a New Color, page 48, but use the same yarn).

Work even for 8 (10) rows.

On each of the next 2 rows, decrease 1 stitch at each end on both boards; work the row. Cut the yarn, leaving an 8-inch-long tail. Lay the tail between the boards and bind off as you did for the finger area.

FINISHING

Fold the thumb in half lengthwise; slide the stitches together on the yarn tail to close the top and then sew the side closed using Invisible Stitch. In the same way, close the top of the fingertip area and sew the side of the mitten closed.

YUMMY PLAID SCARF

A combination of horizontal and vertical stripes knits up as a big plaid that's ideal for a scarf. We've used five yarns in different colors and textures, working two of them together for the background and using the three others for the stripes and end borders. Before you begin, read the chapter Creating Patterns with Color (page 46). If the contrasting yarns become tangled as you work, it's OK to cut them and tie them on again—but don't cut the main color.

SKILL
Advanced

SIZE
Approximately 9 inches wide by 64 inches long

NEEDED
Knitting board, small gauge (30+ needles), with ½ inch between the boards

Knitting hook

Crochet hook, size 5/F

YARN
Assorted textures and weights, including 150 yards each of two sport-weight yarns worked together as one for the main color and 50 yards each of three chunky- or bulky-weight yarns:

Brown Sheep *Top of the Lamb Sport*, 1¾ ounces/50g per skein, each approximately 350 yards/320m (wool): 1 skein #101 Stone (tan) for main color

Plymouth *Baby Alpaca DK*, 1¾ ounces/50g per ball, approximately 125 yards/114m (baby alpaca): 2 balls #100 (off-white) for main color

Rowan *Scottish Tweed Chunky*, 3½ ounces/100g per ball, approximately 109 yards/100m (wool): 1 ball #00016 Thistle (plum)

Plymouth *Encore Chunky*, 3½ ounces/100g per ball, approximately 143 yards/131m (acrylic/wool): 1 ball #999 (maroon)

Brown Sheep *Lamb's Pride Bulky*, 4 ounces/113g per skein, each approximately 125 yards/114m (wool/mohair): 1 skein #M151 Chocolate Souffle (brown)

Or use any same-weight yarns that you like. (Alternatively, use a bulky-weight yarn for the main color and worsted weight for each of the contrasting colors.)

STITCHES
Stockinette (page 27) and Zigzag (page 37)

GAUGE
10 stitches and 12 rows = 3 inches in the plaid pattern (3 stitches and 4 rows = 1 inch in the main color in Stockinette Stitch)

tip:

To work with two yarns for the main color, simply place both skeins together in a large bowl or basket and feed them into the weaving together. Or roll them together into one ball before beginning your project. Either way, be sure to lift both strands as you hook over your stitches.

Scarf

With plum yarn, cast on 30 stitches using the Anchor Yarn method (page 21).

FIRST BORDER

Work 1 row in Stockinette Stitch. Then work 10 rows in Zigzag Stitch. Cut and knot the yarn. Tie on maroon yarn and work 3 rows in Stockinette Stitch.

SET VERTICAL-STRIPE PATTERN

Next row: Weave the following color sequence, tying on each new yarn as needed and weaving the main-color tan sections in Stockinette Stitch. Weave 6 stitches tan, 3 stitches brown, 8 stitches tan, 3 stitches maroon, 4 stitches tan, 2 stitches plum, and 4 stitches tan. Hook over the row.

Work 9 more rows in the vertical-stripe pattern. Cut and knot the plum. Do not cut the tan; lay it aside between needles #2 and #3.

WORK THE PLAID SECTION

Work all the horizontal stripes in Stockinette Stitch with plum yarn. At the end of each vertical-stripe section, cut and knot the plum. Then tie it on at the beginning of each horizontal stripe. Work in the following sequence:

*1 row horizontal stripe in plum.
2 rows vertical-stripe sequence as before.
2 rows horizontal stripe in plum.
12 rows vertical-stripe sequence as before.
1 row horizontal stripe in plum.
10 rows vertical-stripe sequence as before.*

Repeat from * to * 6 more times. Cut and knot the tan.

SECOND BORDER

Next row: Tie on maroon. Work the row in Stockinette Stitch. As you cross each vertical stripe, cut and knot its yarn.

Work 2 more rows in Stockinette Stitch with maroon. Cut and knot the yarn.

Next row: Tie on the plum and work 1 row in Stockinette Stitch.

Work 10 rows in Zigzag Stitch with plum. Remove the scarf from the board using the Firm Crochet (Three-Loop) Bind-Off (page 63). At the cast-on end, Bind Off to Remove the Anchor Yarn using the same Three-Loop method. Pull out the anchor yarn. Pull any yarn tails in between the knit layers.

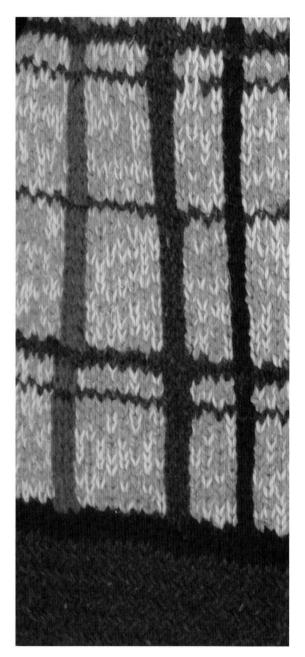

Fabulous
Fashions

What will it be—a smart and handy tote bag, a luxurious shawl, or a striking sweater? Or perhaps a cute pullover for a small tyke you're fond of? There are options for each here, arranged from easiest to most complex.

CLASSIC TOTE

This small tote with Topstitched seams is really cute. Made of seven easy rectangular pieces, it knits up quickly in Stockinette Stitch. For fun, try making the different sections in a variety of pretty colors.

SKILL
Easy

SIZE
Approximately 7 inches high by 8 inches wide and 4 inches deep, not including the handles

NEEDED
Knitting Board, small gauge (22+ needles), with ½ inch between the boards

Knit hook

Crochet hook, size 6/G

Large sewing needle

YARN
Rowan *Big Wool*, 3½ ounces/100g per ball, approximately 87 yards/80m (wool): 3 balls #021 Ice Blue. Or use any superbulky-weight yarn you like.

STITCH
Stockinette (page 27)

GAUGE
3 stitches and 4 rows = 1 inch

Front and Back Panels

Knit 2 alike. For each, cast on 22 stitches using the Anchor Yarn method (page 21). Work in Stockinette Stitch for 23 rows. Remove the panel from the board using the Soft Crochet (Two-Loop) Bind-Off (page 64). At the cast-on end, Bind Off to Remove the Anchor Yarn (page 66); pull out the anchor yarn. Set the front and back panels aside.

Side Panels

Knit 2 alike. For each, cast on 12 stitches using the Anchor Yarn method. Work in Stockinette Stitch for 23 rows. Remove the panel from the board using the Soft Crochet (Two-Loop) Bind-Off. At the cast-on end, Bind Off to Remove the Anchor Yarn; pull out the anchor yarn. Set the side panels aside.

Bottom Panel

Cast on 22 stitches using the Anchor Yarn method. Work in Stockinette Stitch for 12 rows. Remove the panel from the board using the Soft Crochet (Two-Loop) Bind-Off. At the cast-on end, Bind Off to Remove the Anchor Yarn; pull out the anchor yarn. Set the bottom panel aside.

Straps

Knit 2 alike. For each, cast on 6 stitches using the Anchor Yarn method. Work in Stockinette Stitch for 24 rows. Remove the piece from the board using the Soft Crochet (Two-Loop) Bind-Off. At the cast-on end, Bind Off to Remove the Anchor Yarn; pull out the anchor yarn. Set the straps aside.

Finishing

Pin the side panels to the side edges of the front and back panels, making sure the same bound-off edge is at the top on all 4 pieces. Sew the seams using Topstitch (page 81). Pin the bottom panel in place, matching the corners to the seams of the bag; Topstitch in place. Fold each strap in half lengthwise and sew the long edges together using Whipstitch (page 80). Invert a handle, seam down, over the front panel, and pin each end to the top edge about 3 stitches in from a side seam. Whipstitch the handle ends in place. Repeat to sew the second handle to the back panel. Pull any yarn ends in between the knit layers. Your little tote bag is ready to go!

TASSELED SHAWL

Luxurious and lightweight, this airy shawl is really warm and cozy. Treat yourself to a lovely, soft yarn so you can truly appreciate the beauty of the open and lacy double knit.

SKILL
Easy

SIZE
22 inches wide by 75 inches long

NEEDED
Knitting board, small gauge (66+ needles), with 1 inch between the boards

Knit hook

Crochet hook, size 4/F

YARN
Rowan *Scottish Tweed DK*, 1¾ ounces/50g per ball, 123 yards/113m (wool): 17 balls #00004 Stormy Grey. Or use any DK-weight yarn you like.

STITCH
Rib (page 30)

GAUGE
3 stitches and 3 rows = 1 inch

Shawl

Cast on 66 stitches in Rib Stitch using an Anchor Yarn (page 21). Work in Rib Stitch for 225 rows (until the shawl is about 75 inches long). Remove the shawl from the board using the Soft Crochet (Two-Loop) Bind-Off (page 64). At the cast-on edge, Bind Off to Remove the Anchor Yarn (page 66), maintaining the pattern; pull out the anchor yarn. Pull any yarn tails in between the knit layers.

Tassels

Add a tassel to each corner of the shawl (see page 85). For each, wrap the yarn 25 to 30 times around a 7-inch-long piece of cardboard. Cut the yarn at one end of the cardboard and hold the strands together at the other end. Gently open a space between the stitches at the corner of the shawl, thread the yarn through the space, and then fold double, bringing the cut ends together. Secure the strands by wrapping close to the corner with another strand of yarn.

A beautiful turtleneck pullover with simple lines and made in the unique Crisscross Stitch, this is a wonderful project for knitters ready to move beyond easy projects—or for anyone wanting a great-looking classic sweater. You'll learn how to maintain a complex stitch while shaping the knitted pieces. Before beginning, refer to *Increasing and Decreasing in Pattern Stitches* (page 58), being sure to read the paragraph about Crisscross Stitch, so you'll know how to adjust the Weave Pattern as you add and subtract stitches.

DAKOTA SWEATER

SKILL
Intermediate

SIZES
Small (**M**edium, **L**arge, **E**xtra-large)
(see measurements below)

Directions for sizes medium, large, and extra-large appear in parentheses following size small.

DAKOTA SWEATER DIMENSIONS
Measurements are taken with sweater lying flat. All measurements are approximate.

Size	S	M	L	E
Chest (width at underarm)	17"	18"	20"	22"
Hemline (width at hip)	17"	18"	20"	22"
Length (shoulder to hem)	19"	21"	22"	22"
Sleeve (underarm to wrist)	15"	16"	17"	17"

NEEDED
Knitting board, small gauge (80+ needles), with ½ inch between the boards

Knit hook

Crochet hook, size 5/H

Large sewing needle

YARN
Brown Sheep *Lamb's Pride Superwash Worsted*, 3½ ounces/100g per skein, each approximately 200 yards/183m (washable wool): 8 (8,9,9) skeins SW150 Stonewashed Denim. Or use any worsted-weight yarn you like.

STITCH
Crisscross (page 39)

GAUGE
13 stitches and 13 rows = 4 inches

Front and Back
Knit 2 alike. For each, cast on 54 (60,64,70) stitches in Crisscross Stitch, Weave Pattern 1; place an Anchor Yarn (page 21). Work 56 (60,64,64) rows in Crisscross Stitch; end with Weave Pattern 1.

DECREASE FOR ARMHOLES
Next row: Decrease 1 stitch at each end on both boards (see page 58). Work the row, making sure to adjust the beginning of the weave.

Next 2 rows: Work straight as established.

Repeat these 3 rows 27 (30,30,33) more times— for a total of 10 (11,11,12) decrease rows.

SHAPE SHOULDERS AND COLLAR
Before beginning, read Partial Row Bind-off (page 63).

Bind off 4 (4,4,6) stitches at each end on both boards using the Soft Crochet (Two-Loop) Bind-off method (page 64).

For the collar, continue straight as established for 22 more rows. Bind off loosely using the Soft Crochet (Two-Loop) method. At the cast-on edge, Bind Off to Remove the Anchor Yarn (page 66), working loosely. Pull out the anchor yarn.

Sleeves

Knit 2 alike. For each, cast on 30 (34,34,36) stitches in Crisscross Stitch, Weave Pattern 1; place an Anchor Yarn. *Work 8 (9,9,9) rows in Crisscross Stitch. On the next row, increase 1 stitch at each end on both boards; work the row.* Repeat from * to * 2 more times.

Now work 4 (5,6,6) rows as established. On the next row, increase 1 stitch at each end on both boards; work the row. Repeat from ** to ** 5 more times.

Work 1 more row.

DECREASE FOR SLEEVE CAP

Decrease 1 stitch at each end of both boards on every row for 22 (24,24,24) rows. Bind off using the Soft Crochet (Two-Loop) method. At the cast-on edge, Bind Off to Remove the Anchor Yarn, working loosely. Pull out the anchor yarn.

Finishing

Place the front on top of the back, aligning all the edges. Sew the shoulder/collar seams and the side seams with Invisible Stitch (page 79). Fold each sleeve in half lengthwise and sew the underarm seam from the wrist to the first decrease row. Sew a sleeve into each armhole, aligning the underarm seams and easing the top of the sleeve to create a rounded shape. Reinforce the spot where the underarm seams meet (see Reinforcing Weak Spots, page 30). Pull the yarn tails in between the knit layers. Roll the turtleneck down or leave up as desired. What a great, warm winter pullover!

This beautiful shawl offers just enough warmth for a chilly evening. It's made in three sections—two long ones form the fronts and a square hangs in a pretty point between them to form the back. Our sample is made in double-knitting (DK) yarn; if you'd like a heavier yarn, use worsted weight—it will be just a little bit larger and more than a little bit cozier. Before beginning, read Cast On in Pattern (page 25) and Horizontal Stripes (page 47). Also refer to the sidebar Increasing and Decreasing in Pattern Stitches (page 58), being sure to read the paragraph about Open Braid.

MYSTIC SHAWL

SKILL
Intermediate

SIZE
48 inches from back tip to front corner, measured along the outside edge

NEEDED
Knitting board, small gauge (68+ needles) with ½ inch between the boards

Knit hook

Crochet hook, size 4/E or 5/F

Large sewing needle

YARN
Plymouth *Baby Alpaca DK*, 1¾ ounces/50g per ball, 125 yds/114m (baby alpaca) 11 balls #1477 green (main color), 3 balls #4145 blue. Or use any DK-weight yarn you like.

STITCH
Open Braid (page 34)

GAUGE
5 stitches and 4 rows = 1 inch

Note: Work entirely in Open Braid Stitch. Leave the main-color yarn attached while working the contrasting stripes. When you begin each contrasting stripe, tie on the yarn at needle #2 (see Tying on a New Color, page 48). When the stripe is complete, cut and knot the contrasting yarn, leaving a 3-inch-long tail.

Front Panels

Knit 2 alike. For each, with the green yarn, cast on 60 stitches in Open Braid Stitch using an Anchor Yarn (page 21). Work 12 rows.

Tie on the blue yarn; work 2 rows.

Pick up the green; work 18 rows.

Tie on the blue; work 4 rows.

Pick up the green; work 20 rows.

Tie on the blue; work 6 rows.

Pick up the green; work 10 rows.

Remove the knitting from the board using the Soft Crochet (Two-Loop) Bind-Off (page 64); work loosely. (Because of the seams required to finish this shawl, we don't recommend binding off in pattern.) At the cast-on edge, Bind Off to Remove the Anchor Yarn (page 66); work loosely. Pull out the anchor yarn.

Back Panel

With the green yarn, cast on 68 stitches in Open Braid Stitch using an Anchor Yarn. Work 8 rows.

Tie on the blue yarn; work 4 rows.

Pick up the green; work 18 rows.

Tie on the blue; work 3 rows.

Pick up the green; work 18 rows.

Tie on the blue; work 3 rows.

DECREASE FOR NECKLINE

On each of the next 8 rows, decrease 1 stitch at the right end on both boards and then work the row. Maintain the Open Braid Stitch pattern as you decrease.

As you did for the front pieces, remove the knitting from the board and bind off at the cast-on edge.

Pull out the anchor yarn.

Finishing

The 12-row green ends of the front panels are the loose ends; the 10-row ends join the back, one on each side of the neckline. Referring to the back-view photo on page 151, arrange the pieces on a large table: Align one end of each front panel with an edge of the back—the neckline edge should be in between the front panels. Using Invisible Stitch (page 79), sew the pieces together. Tuck any yarn tails in between the knit layers. Put on the shawl and toss one end over the opposite shoulder—very smart!

tip:

One of the seams joins a side edge to a bound-off edge. It's easier to make this seam if you baste the pieces together first— this keeps the side edge from stretching.

Here's a warm and stylish jacket that goes well with jeans or casual dressy attire. Accented with stripes and Open Rib Stitch, the jacket has three-quarter-length sleeves and a short body that give it a bold look. The front placket bands are knit separately, so the stitches run perpendicular to the body. This project is complex but not very complicated, so give it a whirl in a sporty yarn, as shown, or go for something dressier. Before you begin, read the chapter Creating Patterns with Color (page 46), being sure to read Horizontal Stripes (page 47).

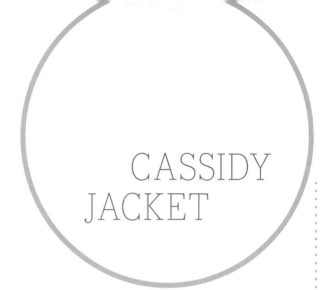

CASSIDY JACKET

SKILL
Advanced

SIZES
Small (**M**edium, **L**arge)

Directions for sizes medium and large appear in parentheses following size small.

CASSIDY JACKET DIMENSIONS
Measurements are taken with sweater lying flat. All measurements are approximate.

Size	S	M	L
Chest (width at underarm)	17"	19"	21"
Hemline (width at hip)	15"	17"	19"
Length (neckline to hem)	17"	18"	20"
Sleeve (underarm to cuff)	10"	12"	14"

NEEDED
Knitting board, small gauge (60+ needles), with ½ inch between the boards

Knit hook

Crochet hook, size 5/F or 6/G

Large sewing needle

Five ¾-inch diameter buttons

YARN
Ironstone *Harmony*, 1¾ ounces/50g per skein, approximately 110 yards/101m (wool): 8 (10,10) skeins #16173 (red heather) for the main color; 1 skein #16171 (yellow-green) for the stripes. Or use any bulky-weight yarn you like.

STITCHES
Stockinette (page 27), Open Rib (page 32), and Rib (page 30)

GAUGE
5 stitches and 7 rows = 2 inches in Stockinette Stitch

Back
With red yarn, cast on 50 (54,60) stitches using the Anchor Yarn method (page 21).

BOTTOM BORDER
Work the border in Open Rib Stitch; leave the red attached while you work the contrast stripes:

Work 2 rows in red.

Tie on yellow-green yarn and work 2 rows; do not cut the yarn.

Pick up the red and work 2 rows.

Pick up the yellow-green and work 2 rows; cut the yarn, leaving a 3-inch-long tail.

Pick up the red and work 2 more rows.

Body
Work the body in Stockinette Stitch. First, on the side of the board that has the Open Rib surface, lift 1 loop from each needle that has 2 loops, and transfer it to the empty needle to its left—there is now 1 loop on each needle on each board. Work 1 row.

Next row: Increase 1 stitch at each end on both boards (see page 55); work the row.

Work 20 (22, 24) rows.

Next row: Increase 1 stitch at each end on both boards; work the row.

Work 6 rows (all sizes).

DECREASE FOR ARMHOLES

Next row: Decrease 1 stitch at each end on both boards (see page 59). Work the row in Stockinette Stitch.

Next 2 rows: Work straight as established in Stockinette Stitch.

Repeat these 3 rows 11 (12,14) times—for a total of 12 (13,15) decrease rows.

SHAPE SHOULDERS

Before beginning, read Partial Row Bind-off (page 63).

Next row: Bind off 5 stitches at each end on both boards using the Soft Crochet (Two-Loop) Bind-Off (page 64)—20 (22,24) stitches remain; work the row in Stockinette Stitch.

KNIT THE COLLAR

Work the collar in Open Rib Stitch, using the same stripe sequence as on the bottom border. Make sure you use the same side of the board for the Open Rib as you did before. When the final 2 rows of the main color are complete, remove the back from the board using the Soft Crochet (Two-Loop) Bind-Off. At the cast-on edge, Bind Off to Remove the Anchor Yarn (page 66), being sure to maintain the pattern (see Bind Off in Pattern, page 65). Pull out the anchor yarn.

Fronts

Knit the right and left fronts alike but work the Open Rib Stitch on the back board for one of them—the shaping on each piece will mirror the other when you turn them both Open Rib–side up. With the red yarn, cast on 20 (24,28) stitches using the Anchor Yarn method.

BOTTOM BORDER AND BODY

Work as for the back.

DECREASE FOR ARMHOLE

Work as for the back, but decrease at the left end only on both boards.

SHAPE SHOULDER AND CAST ON FOR COLLAR

At the left end of the board only, bind off 5 stitches as you did for the back. Weave the row in Stockinette Stitch; when you reach the end, continue weaving to add 6 stitches (these will sit at the top of the button and buttonhole bands when the sweater is finished). Lay an anchor yarn over the new stitches. Do not hook over.

KNIT THE COLLAR

Work as for the back collar

Button Band

With the red yarn, cast on 50 (52,56) stitches in Rib Stitch using an Anchor Yarn. Work 5 rows in Rib Stitch. Remove the band from the board using the Firm Crochet (Three-Loop) Bind-Off (page 63), being sure to maintain the pattern.

Buttonhole Band

Before you begin, refer to the photo and use the button band to plan the spacing for the buttonholes. Cast on 50 (52,56) stitches as you did for the button band. According to your spacing plan, mark the front of the board with tape to indicate the needles that will be used for the buttonholes.

Work 2 rows in Rib Stitch.

Next row, work buttonholes following the directions for Buttonholes Without Placket Band (page 71).

Work 2 more rows in Rib Stitch. Bind off as for the button band.

Sleeves

Make 2 alike. For each, with red yarn, cast on 34 (38,40) stitches in Open Rib Stitch using an Anchor Yarn. Work the bottom border as for the back. Change to Stockinette Stitch and work 28 (32,34) rows.

DECREASE FOR SLEEVE CAP

Next row: Decrease 1 stitch at each end on both boards (see page 59). Work the row in Stockinette Stitch.

Next 2 rows: Work straight as established in Stockinette Stitch.

Repeat these 3 rows 12 (14,15) times—for a total of 13 (15,16) decrease rows. Then decrease 1 stitch at each end on both boards every row until 4 stitches remain. Remove the sleeve from the board and bind off to remove the anchor yarn as for the back.

Finishing

Make sure the Open Rib Stitch faces out on all pieces. Match the stripes and use Invisible Stitch (page 79) for all seams. First sew the button band to the left front (as worn), joining the top of the band to the collar extension. Sew the buttonhole band to the right front in the same way. Next place the fronts on top of the back, aligning all edges. Sew the shoulder/collar seams. Sew the underarm seams. Then fold each sleeve in half lengthwise; sew the underarm seam from the wrist to the first decrease row. Sew a sleeve into each armhole, aligning the underarm seams and easing the top of the sleeve to create a rounded shape. Reinforce the spot where the underarm seams meet (see Reinforcing Weak Spots, page 30). Overlap the placket bands and sew a button opposite each buttonhole (page 70). Pull the yarn tails in between the knit layers. Your Cassidy Jacket is ready to wear!

LITTLE CHICK SWEATER

If you have a little one to take out into the cold, you will love this adorable sweater with its cute running-chick motif. You may take your choice of Crisscross Stitch or Rib Stitch for the hem and wrist borders. Before you begin, read the chapter Creating Patterns with Color (page 46), being sure to read the sidebar Charted Designs (page 52).

SKILL
Advanced

SIZES
Toddler **S**mall (**M**edium)

Directions for sizes medium appear in parentheses following size small.

LITTLE CHICK SWEATER DIMENSIONS
Measurements are taken with sweater lying flat. All measurements are approximate.

Toddler Size	Small	Medium
Chest (width at underarm)	11"	13"
Hemline (width at hip)	10"	12"
Length (neckline to hem)	11"	11"
Sleeve (underarm to wrist)	5"	6"

NEEDED
Knitting board, small gauge (30+ needles), with ½ inch between the boards

Knit hook

Crochet hook, size 5/F

Large sewing needle

YARN
Plymouth *Baby Alpaca Grande*, 3½ ounces/100g per ball, approximately 110 yards/101m (baby alpaca): 3 balls #2271 (maroon) for the main color; 1 ball #779 (soft green) for the accents. Or use any bulky-weight yarn you like.

STITCHES
Stockinette (page 27), Rib (page 30), and Crisscross (page 39)

GAUGE
5 stitches and 6 rows = 2 inches in Stockinette Stitch

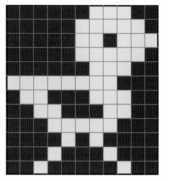

LITTLE CHICK CHART

Front

Using contrasting-color (soft green) yarn, cast on 30 (34) stitches using the Anchor Yarn method (page 21). Work 4 rows in Crisscross Stitch. Cut and knot the yarn.

Tie on the maroon yarn (see Tying on a New Color, page 48). Work 4 (6) rows in Stockinette Stitch.

Next row, begin the chick: Following the graph above, work the first stitches of the chick motif in soft green, placing the rear foot on needle #12 (#13). Then work the remaining stitches of the row with maroon in Stockinette Stitch.

Continue in this manner to complete the chick motif. Then work 5 (7) more rows in Stockinette Stitch with maroon only.

tip:

You can work the
borders in Rib Stitch instead
of Crisscross—choose
whichever you wish.

DECREASE FOR ARMHOLES AND DIVIDE FOR NECK OPENING

Mark the center of the knitting by placing colored tape on the front of your knitting board and marking the tape between needles #15 and #16 (#17 and #18) with a pen. Tie on a second skein of maroon to the right of center so that you can work both halves of the top at the same time. On both boards, transpose the 2 stitches on the left of the center mark with the 2 stitches on the right (see Reinforcing Weak Spots, page 30).

Next row: Decrease 1 stitch at each end on both boards (see page 59). Work the row in Stockinette Stitch, making sure to use the specific yarn for each half, and working a 2-stitch placket on each side of the neck opening (see Slash-Pocket Placket Bands, page 75). (The placket will give the vertical edges more stability once the drawstring is added.)

Next row: Work straight as established.

Repeat these 2 rows 5 (6) times more.

SHAPE SHOULDERS AND WORK NECKBAND

Before beginning, read Partial Row Bind-off (page 63).

Bind off 2 (3) stitches at each end on both boards.

Work 4 rows in Rib Stitch. Working loosely, remove the front from the board using the Soft Crochet (Two-Loop) Bind-Off (page 64). At the cast-on edge, Bind Off to Remove the Anchor Yarn (page 66); work loosely and maintain the pattern (see Bind Off in Pattern, page 66). Pull out the anchor yarn.

Back

Work the back the same as the front—but do not work the chick motif or divide the knitting for the neck.

Sleeves

Knit 2 alike. For each, using soft green, cast on 18 (22) stitches using the Anchor Yarn method. Work 4 rows in Crisscross Stitch. Cut and knot the yarn. Tie on the maroon yarn. Work the remainder of the sleeve in Stockinette Stitch.

Next row: Increase 1 stitch at each end on both boards (see page 55); work the row.

Next row: Work straight as established.

Repeat these 2 rows 3 (4) more times. Then work straight for 2 more rows (both sizes).

DECREASE FOR SLEEVE CAP

Next row: Decrease 1 stitch at each end on both boards; work the row.

Repeat this row until only 2 stitches remain. Remove the sleeve from the board and bind off at the cuff as you did for the other pieces.

Finishing

Place the front on top of the back, aligning all the edges. Sew the shoulder seams and the side seams with Invisible Stitch (page 79). Fold each sleeve in half lengthwise and sew the underarm seam from the wrist to the first decrease row. Sew a sleeve into each armhole, aligning the underarm seams and easing the top of the sleeve to create a rounded shape. Reinforce the spot where the underarm seams meet. Pull the yarn tails in between the knit layers.

TIE

Refer to Drawstrings and Ties (page 83) to crochet a 20- to 30-inch-long tie. Using the crochet hook, thread the tie shoelace-fashion between the stitches along the neck opening; place the middle of the tie at the bottom of the opening. When you are done, knot each end of the tie several times to form a small ball and conceal the yarn ends. How cute is this?

Hood up or hood down, this is a great little sweater that will keep your favorite toddler nice and warm. Before you begin, read the chapter Creating Patterns with Color (page 46), being sure to read the section Horizontal Stripes (page 47) and the section on Cables (pages 41–45).

SKILL
Advanced

SIZE
Toddler Large

For a taller child, make the body and sleeves longer.

HUCKLEBERRY PULLOVER DIMENSIONS
Measurements are taken with sweater lying flat. All measurements are approximate.

Toddler Size	Large
Chest (width at underarm)	14"
Hemline (width at hip)	13"
Length (shoulder to hem)	16"
Shoulders (width across upper back)	13"
Sleeve (shoulder to wrist)	13"

NEEDED
Knitting board, small gauge (44+ needles), with ½ inch between the boards

Knit hook

Crochet hook, size 5/F

Large sewing needle

2 stitch holders for cable stitches

YARN
Plymouth *Baby Alpaca Grande*, 3½ ounces/100g per ball, approximately 110 yards/101m (baby alpaca): 12 balls #799 (soft green) for the main color; 2 balls #365 (blue) for the stripes. Or use any bulky-weight yarn you like.

STITCHES
Rib (page 30), Ribbed Cables (page 43), and Open Rib (page 32)

GAUGE
5 stitches and 6 rows = 2 inches in Rib Stitch

Cable Pattern

The cable sections are worked on 3 ribs (6 stitches) each, with 4 rows of Rib Stitch following each Cable Twist row. The cable sections are on needles #11 through #16 and needles #25 through #30 for the sweater front. Mark the knitting board with tape to indicate these needles after you cast on. Work each cable section as follows: count the ribs from left to right within each section and transpose the stitches before you weave the row.

Twist 1: Transpose rib 2 with rib 3, placing rib 2 in front.

Twist 2: Transpose rib 1 with rib 2, placing rib 2 in front.

After working both twists for the first time as indicated in the sweater directions, *work 4 rows in Rib Stitch, 1 row with Twist 1 in the cable sections, 4 rows in Rib Stitch, and 1 row with Twist 2 in the cable sections*. Repeat from * to * while at the same time following the remainder of the directions to shape the front.

Front

With blue yarn, cast on 44 stitches in Rib Stitch using an Anchor Yarn (page 21). Work 6 rows in Open Rib Stitch. (Work the remainder of the front entirely in Rib Stitch, twisting the cables when indicated.)

Row 7: Tie on soft-green yarn (leave the blue attached) and work the row.

Row 8—first cable row: Continue with soft green, working Cable Twist 1 on each marked set of needles.

Rows 9 through 12: Work 1 more row with the soft green. Pick up the blue (leave the soft green attached) and work 2 rows. Cut and knot the blue. Work 1 row with the soft green.

Row 13—second cable row: Continue with the soft green, working Cable Twist 2 in each marked set of needles.

Using the soft green only and continuing in the cable pattern as indicated on page 65, work 19 more rows.

DECREASE FOR ARMHOLES

Before beginning, read the sidebar Increasing or Decreasing Pattern Stitches (page 000).

Work 13 rows, decreasing 1 stitch at each end on both boards on the first and then every other row—30 stitches remain. Make sure to maintain the Rib pattern and Cable sequence as you decrease.

DIVIDE FOR NECK OPENING

First locate the center (between the second and third Ribs between the cable sections).

Tie on a second skein of soft green to the right of center, so that you can work both halves of the top at the same time. On both boards, transpose the Rib on the left of center with the rib on the right of center (see Reinforcing Weak Spots, page 30).

Work 6 more rows, making sure to use the specific yarn for each half; continue to decrease at the armhole edge on every other row and twist the cables when appropriate—24 stitches remain. Work straight for 2 more rows.

Working loosely, remove the front from the board using the Soft Crochet (Two-Loop) Bind-Off (page 64). At the cast-on edge, Bind Off to Remove the Anchor Yarn (page 66); work loosely. Pull out the anchor yarn.

Back

Work the back the same as the front, but do not divide the knitting for the neck opening; omit the cables or work them, whichever you prefer.

Sleeves

Knit 2 alike. For each, with blue, cast on 24 stitches in Rib Stitch using an Anchor Yarn. Work 6 rows in Open Rib Stitch. Then, on the side of the board that has the Open Rib surface, lift 1 loop from each needle that has 2 loops and transfer it to the empty needle to its left—there is now 1 loop on each needle on each board.

Tie on the soft green (leave the blue attached) and work 2 rows in regular Rib Stitch.

Pick up the blue (leave the soft green attached) and work 2 rows in Rib Stitch. Cut and knot the blue.

Continuing in Rib Stitch with soft green, work 20 more rows.

DECREASE FOR SLEEVE CAP

Maintain the Rib pattern as you decrease.

Next 8 rows: Decrease 1 stitch at each end on both boards; work the row.

Work 1 row straight as established.

Next 2 rows: Decrease 1 stitch at each end on both boards; work the row.

Work 1 row straight as established.

Next row: Decrease 1 stitch at each end on both boards; work the row—2 stitches remain.

Remove the sleeve from the board and bind off at the cuff as you did for the other pieces.

Hood

With soft green, cast on 28 stitches in Rib Stitch using an Anchor Yarn. Work 60 rows in Rib Stitch. Remove the hood from the board and bind off at the cast-on edge as you did for the other pieces.

Finishing

Use Invisible Stitch (page 79) for all seams except the casing. Place the front on top of the back, aligning all the edges. Sew the side seams. Sew the shoulder seams for 1 inch starting at the armhole edge. Fold each sleeve in half lengthwise and sew the underarm seam from the wrist to the first decrease row. Sew a sleeve into each armhole, aligning the underarm seams and easing the top of the sleeve to create a rounded shape. Reinforce the spot where the underarm seams meet (see Reinforcing Weak Spots, page 30).

On one long edge of the hood, fold over one complete rib to become a casing for the Drawstring; sew the edge down using small Topstitches (page 81). Then fold the hood in half crosswise and sew the edges opposite the casing together using Invisible Stitch. Referring to the photo, position the bottom of the hood on the neck edge of the body—make sure the casing is on the outside and align the back seam with the center of the back neck edge. Sew the hood in place, leaving the casing open on the outside at both ends.

DRAWSTRING

Refer to Drawstrings and Ties (page 83) to crochet a 38-inch-long drawstring with soft green.

Affix a large safety pin to one end and thread it through the casing; remove the pin. So cute!

NEWBERRY PULLOVER

What a great sweater this is: so classy. Two natural colors, textured borders, and a simple floral motif tossed with apparent random on the front, back, and sleeves make it cozy to wear and fun to knit. It's styled with drop shoulders, a funnel collar, and super-long sleeves that you can turn up into deep cuffs. This is detail an advanced knitter will enjoy from start to finish. Before you begin, read the chapter Creating Patterns with Color (page 46), being sure to read the sidebar Charted Designs (page 52)

SKILL
Advanced

SIZES
Small (**M**edium, **L**arge)

Directions for sizes medium and large appear in parentheses following size small.

NEWBERRY PULLOVER DIMENSIONS
Measurements are taken with sweater lying flat. All measurements are approximate.

Size	S	M	L
Chest (width at underarm)	17"	19"	22"
Hemline (width at hip)	17"	19"	22"
Length (neckline to hem)	17"	20"	21"
Shoulders (width across upper back)	17"	19"	22"
Sleeve (shoulder to wrist)	22"	24"	25"

NEEDED
Knitting board, small gauge (70+ needles), with ½ inch between the boards

Knit hook

Crochet hook, size 4/E or 5/F

Large sewing needle

YARN
Nashua *Creative Focus Chunky*, 3½ ounces/100g per ball, approximately 110 yards/100m (wool/alpaca): 12 (14,14) balls #0100 Natural (cream) for the main color; 4 balls #0289 Earth Heather (taupe) for the accents.

STITCHES
Stockinette (page 27) and Crisscross (page 39)

GAUGE
3 stitches and 4 rows = 1 inch

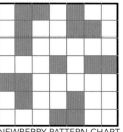

NEWBERRY PATTERN CHART

Note: Each time you begin the floral motif, work the two contrast stitches of the first row of the graph on the needles indicated by number in the project directions. In other words, if the directions say to begin on needles #14 and #15, count from the left end of the board and work one contrast stitch on needle #14 and one on needle #15. Then follow the graph to place the contrast stitches on the subsequent rows.

Front and Back

Knit 2 alike. For each, with taupe yarn cast on 52 (60,68) stitches using the Anchor Yarn method (page 21). Work 24 (26,28) rows in Crisscross Stitch. Cut and knot the yarn. Tie on cream yarn (see Tying on a New Color, page 48). Work 6 (12,16) rows in Stockinette Stitch.

*Next row, begin a floral motif: Following the graph above, work the first stitches of the floral motif in taupe on needles #14 and #15. Then work the remaining stitches of the row with cream in Stockinette Stitch.

Next 6 rows: Continue in this manner to complete the floral motif. Cut and knot the taupe yarn.*

With cream yarn, work 0 (2,4) rows in Stockinette Stitch.

Second motif: Repeat from * to *, beginning the motif on needles #33 and #34 (#41 and #42, #47 and #48).

With cream, work 4 rows in Stockinette Stitch (all sizes).

Third motif: Repeat from * to *, beginning the motif on needles #24 and #25 (#24 and #25, #26 and #27).

With main color, work 4 rows in Stockinette Stitch (all sizes).

Fourth motif: Repeat from * to *, beginning the motif on needles #36 and #37 (#47 and #48, #53 and #54).

With main color, work 4 rows in Stockinette Stitch (all sizes).

Fifth motif: Repeat from * to *, beginning the motif on needles #7 and #8 (#9 and #10, #11 and #12).

With main color, work 1 (2,4) rows in Stockinette Stitch.

SHAPE SHOULDERS AND WORK COLLAR

Before beginning, read Partial Row Bind-off (page 63).

Using the Soft Crochet (Two-Loop) Bind-off method (page 64), bind off 12 (14, 18) stitches at each end on both boards—28 (32,32) stitches remain. Work the row in Stockinette Stitch.

Next, for the collar, work 12 (16,16) rows in Crisscross Stitch.

Remove the piece from the board using the Soft Crochet (Two-Loop) Bind-Off. At the cast-on edge, Bind Off to Remove the Anchor Yarn (page 66), maintaining the pattern (see Bind Off in Pattern, page 65). Pull out the anchor yarn.

Sleeves

Knit 2 alike. For each, with taupe cast on 30 (34,36) stitches using the Anchor Yarn method. Work 24 (26,28) rows in Crisscross Stitch. Cut and knot the yarn. Tie on the cream. Work 6 (8,8) rows in Stockinette Stitch.

First motif: Repeat from * to *, beginning the motif on needles #8 and #9 (#10 and #11, #12 and #13).

First increase sequence: On the next row, increase 1 stitch at each end on both boards (see page 58) and then work the row in Stockinette Stitch. Work straight as established for 6 (8,8) rows. Then increase 1 stitch on each end on both boards and work another row.**

Second motif: Repeat from * to *, beginning the motif on needles #24 and #25 (#26 and #27, #27 and #28).

Second increase sequence: Repeat from ** to ** to work another set of increases.

Third motif: Repeat from * to *, beginning the motif on needles #13 and #14 (#13 and #14, #16 and #17).

Third increase sequence: On the next row, increase 1 stitch at each end on both boards and then work the row in Stockinette Stitch. Work straight as established for 8 (10,10) rows.

Sizes medium and large only: On the next 7 rows work a fourth motif, beginning on needles #26 and #27 (medium) or #27 and #28 (large). Then, with cream, work 2 (6) rows in Stockinette Stitch.

BIND OFF

Remove the sleeve from the board and bind off at the cuff as you did for the front and back.

Finishing

Use Invisible Stitch (page 79) for all seams and change the sewing-yarn color to match each knitted area. Remember there is no wrong or right side to the knitting and the motifs will fall in different places depending on which side faces out, so you may wish to lay everything out before sewing any seams. Place the front on top of the back, aligning all the edges. Sew the shoulder/collar seams. Lay the sweater flat again. Fold the sleeves in half lengthwise and position them on each side of the sweater. Mark the middle of the top edge of the sleeve by pulling a short piece of yarn through it with a crochet hook. Then pull the yarn through the shoulder seam on the body and tie to temporarily secure the alignment. Sew the top of each sleeve to the side of the body, making sure that the underarm edges all fall at the same distance below the shoulder seam. Now sew each side/underarm seam from hem to wrist. Pull the yarn tails in between the knit layers. Don your pullover and turn up the cuffs as you wish.

RUGBEE
TOTE BAG

What a great big bag for carrying just about anything —how about your knitting board and yarn? Or save a tree and tote your groceries in it. If you're eager for a multicolor challenge, this is the perfect project. The charts show the entire width of the bag, so it's easy to keep track of your weaving. The strap can be made any length you like. Before you begin, read the chapter Creating Patterns with Color (page 46), being sure to read the section on Horizontal Stripes (page 47) and the sidebar Charted Designs (page 52).

SKILL
Advanced

SIZE
16 inches high by 16 inches wide by 2½ inches deep; strap shown is 45 inches long above bag

NEEDED
Knitting board, small gauge (52+ needles), with ½ inch between the boards

Knit hook

Crochet hook, size 6/G

Large sewing needle

1 large button (1 to 1½ inches in diameter), optional

YARN
Brown Sheep *Lamb's Pride Bulky*, 4 ounces/113g per skein, each approximately 125 yards/114m (wool/mohair blend): 4 skeins #M07 Sable (brown); 4 skeins #M03 Grey Heather (gray); 4 skeins #M162 Mulberry (maroon); 1 skein #M11 White Frost (white). Or use any bulky-weight yarn you like. (You need 300 yards each of brown, maroon, and gray, and about 50 yards of white.)

STITCH
Stockinette (page 27)

GAUGE
5 stitches and 7 rows = 2 inches

Note: The bag is worked entirely in Stockinette Stitch. To minimize tangling, each time you finish a row with white yarn, cut it and tie off. Then tie on again the next time you need it.

Front Panel

With brown yarn, cast on 52 stitches using the Anchor Yarn method (page 21). Work 2 rows. Leave the brown attached and change to gray; work 2 rows. Leave the gray attached and tie on maroon for the next row.

WORK THE FIRST DIAMOND PATTERN

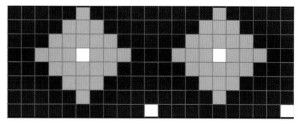

Referring to the first row of Chart 1 (above) and counting from the left end of the board, tie on white yarn at needle #11. Weave the multicolor pattern shown for Row 1; hook over. Work the remaining 7 rows of the chart.

Work Chart 1 three more times.

tip:

If the yarns become annoyingly tangled, simply cut and tie one of them; then, tie it on again at the next needle where you need it.

WORK THE SECOND DIAMOND PATTERN

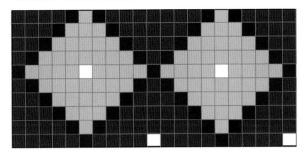

In the same way, work the 10 rows of Chart 2 (above) twice.

WORK THE THIRD DIAMOND PATTERN

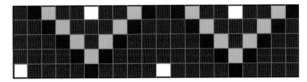

And to finish the Diamond section of the panel, work the 5 rows of Chart 3 (above) once. Cut and tie the maroon and white yarns after working the last stitch of each.

TOP BORDER

Work 1 row in gray; cut and tie the gray. Work 2 rows in brown. Remove the panel from the board using the Soft Crochet (Two-Loop) Bind-Off (page 64). At the cast-on edge, Bind Off to Remove the Anchor Yarn (page 66); pull out the anchor yarn.

Back Panel

Knit the back panel the same as the front. Or cast on and work a total of 68 rows in a single color and then bind off.

Strap

With brown yarn, cast on 8 stitches using the Anchor Yarn method.

WORK THE STRIPE PATTERN

Work 3 rows in brown.

Tie on the gray and lay the brown between needles #2 and #3, counting from the left end of the board.

Work 3 rows in gray.

Tie on the maroon and lay the gray between needles #1 and #2.

Work 3 rows in maroon.

Lay the maroon between needles #1 and #2.

Picking up each color as needed, repeat this 9-row stripe sequence until the strap is the desired length (it must be about 50 inches long to go around the sides and bottom of the bag, plus whatever you want for a shoulder strap).

Remove the strap from the board using the Soft Crochet (Two-Loop) Bind-Off. At the cast-on edge, Bind Off to Remove the Anchor Yarn; pull out the anchor yarn.

Button Tab (Optional) made separately

With brown yarn, cast on 9 stitches in Stockinette Stitch using the Anchor Yarn method (page 21).

Work 5 rows in St St.

Next row, work a buttonhole at needle #5 following directions for Buttonhole in Placket Band (page 70)

Work 20 more rows in St St.

Bind off using Soft Crochet (two-loop) Bind Off. At the cast-on edge draw the anchor yarn to gather the 9 stitches together. Tie securely. Trim yarn ends and tuck into knitting.

Finishing

Using Invisible Stitch (page 79), sew the ends of the strap together to make a ring. Positioning the seam in the middle of the bottom edge of the back panel (the cast-on edge), pin one edge of the strap to the bottom of the panel. Then turn the strap gently around each corner and pin to the side edges. Sew together using Invisible Stitch. At each top corner, double back or make a couple of Whipstitches (page 80) for reinforcement. Now pin the front panel to the other edge of the strap; on each side, make sure the top edges and bottom corners align across the strap. Sew the front panel to the strap. Pull any yarn tails in between the knit layers.

Sew Button Tab to bag back. Sew button to bag front, using Button Tab for proper placement.

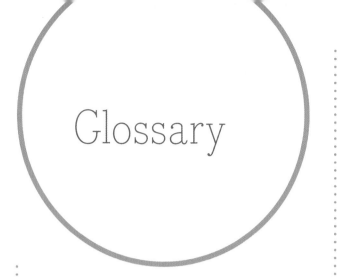

Glossary

Anchor Yarn
A contrast piece of yarn used to secure the initial row of cast on stitches, also used to assist in moving the initial rows of knitting down between the knitting boards.

Back Board
The board farthest away from the knitter is referred to as the Back Board. A knitting board is made up of a pair of boards studded with pegs or needles.

Bind Off Row
The last row in the knitting process, used to remove the completed piece from the knitting board while creating a finished edge.

Bind Off at Anchor Yarn
The anchor yarn stays in the knitting until the piece is completed or the anchor yarn is removed. At that point the cast on stitches are bound off to make a finished edge. The anchor yarn may be removed after the bind off is completed.

Cast On
The first step in the knitting process. Stitches or loops are made around the pegs on the knitting board. There are several methods that can be used, but it is not considered a knitted row.

Circular
The process of weaving the yarn over the pegs or needles, first on the back board from the left hand side of the board to the right hand side of the board, and back again on the front board to the beginning of the row. Some stitch patterns complete a full circular with just one pass on the board or from left to right without returning to the start.

Decrease
The process of reducing the number of stitches on the knitting board, making the piece narrower across the width.

Double-Sided Knitting
A type of knitted fabric made by working on two sets of needles on parallel knitting boards to create a double thickness of fabric joined by interlocking stitches. The resulting fabric is reversible with no front or back side.

Double Stitch
A knitted stitch which requires two needles with the yarn wrapped simultaneously around each. Both sides of the stitch are interlocked with one another.

Front Board
The board closest to the knitter is referred to as the Front Board. A knitting board is made up of a pair of boards studded with pegs.

Gauge
The amount of stitches and rows in one or more inches of knitted fabric. Gauge guides are available that help measure the stitches and rows.

Hook Over
The process of lifting the lower loops over the top of the needles to make a row of knitting. Once all needles on the row have been Hooked Over, the row moves down and the knitter can start the next row by weaving the yarn in the selected stitch pattern.

Increase
The process of adding more stitches on the knitting board, making the piece wider across the width.

Loop Knot
The initial stitch placed on the first needle when starting a new piece. It is formed by folding the end of the working yarn on to itself to make a slip knot about the diameter of pencil or the size of the stitches to be knit.

Stitch Pattern
The pattern or path of weaving the yarn on the pegs or needles results in different types of stitches.

Swatch
A test piece of knitting using the yarn intended for the pattern. It is usually knit over 10 stitches and 10 rows and used to check the intended gauge, as well to preview how the pattern looks in the chosen yarn.

Weaving
The process of laying the yarn across the needles in various patterns.

Working Yarn
The main yarn that is attached to the knitting, used to work the stitches.

Yarn tail
The 2- to 3-inch end of yarn that extends from the initial loop knot or the closing knot. Generally these ends are woven back into the finished piece.

Resources

KNITTING BOARDS AND LOOMS

Authentic Knitting Board
60 Carysbrook Road
Fork Union, VA 23055
www.knittingboard.com
info@knittingboard.com

Provo Craft
151 East 3450 North
Spanish Fork, UT 84660
www.provocraft.com

NOTIONS

Coats & Clark
Consumer Services
P.O. Box 12229
Greenville, SC 29612
www.coatsandclark.com

YARN SHOP

Seed Stitch
21 Front Street
Salem, MA 01970
www.seedstitchfineyarn.com

YARNS

Bernat Yarns
320 Livingstone Ave South
Listowel, Ontario, Canada
www.bernat.com

Brown Sheep Company
100662 County Road 16
Mitchell, NE 69357
www.brownsheep.com

Ironstone Yarns
5401 San Diego NE
Albuqueque, NM 87113
www.ironstoneonline.com

Lion Brand
135 Kero Road
Carlstadt, NJ 07072
www.lionbrand.com

Nashua Handknits
165 Ledge Street
Nashua, NH 03060
www.nashuaknits.com

Patons Yarns
320 Livingstone Avenue South
Listowel, Ontario, Canada
N4W3H3
www.patonsyarn.com

Plymouth Yarn Co.
500 Layfayette Street
Bristol, PA 19007
www.plymouthyarn.com

Reynolds Yarns
A Division of JCA
35 Scales Lane
Townsend, MA 01469
www.jcacrafts.com

Rowan Yarns
Westminster Fibers
8 Shelter Drive
Greer, SC 29650
www.knitrowan.com
info@westminsterfibers.com

Index